100 WALKS IN Dorset

compiled by

**Norman Amey,
Peter Clarke,
Don Pallister
&
Andrew Welch**

D1407290

The Crowood Press

First published in 1995 by
The Crowood Press Ltd
Ramsbury
Marlborough
Wiltshire SN8 2HR

www.crowood.com

This impression 2008

British Library Cataloguing-in-Publication Data
A catalogue record for this book is
available from the British Library

ISBN 978 1 85223 848 3

All maps by Janet Powell

Typeset by Carreg Limited, Ross-on-Wye, Herefordshire

Printed and bound in Great Britain by CPI Antony Rowe, Chippenham, Wiltshire

CONTENTS

35.	Stinsford	$4^1/_2$m	(7km)
36.	White Horse Hill	$4^1/_2$m	(7km)
37.	Tarrant Keyneston	5m	(8km)
38.	Bere Regis and Turners Puddle	5m	(8km)
39.	Uplyme	5m	(8km)
40.	Fiddleford Mill	5m	(8km)
41.	The Piddle Valley	5m	(8km)
42.	Marshwood and Bettiscombe	5m	(8km)
43.	Coney's Castle	5m	(8km)
44.	Melbury Sampford	5m	(8km)
45.	Badbury Rings	$5^1/_2$m	(9km)
46.	Chalbury Hill and Horton	$5^1/_2$m	(9km)
47.	Longham and the River Stour	$5^1/_2$m	($8^1/_2$km)
48.	Alderholt and Cranborne Common	$5^1/_2$m	(9km)
49.	St Aldhelm's Head	$5^1/_2$m	(9km)
50.	Kimmeridge Cliff and Swyre Head	$5^1/_2$m	(9km)
51.	Cheddington	$5^1/_2$m	(9km)
52.	Toller Porcorum	$5^1/_2$m	(9km)
53.	Dorsetshire Gap	$5^1/_2$m	(9km)
54.	Puddletown Forest	$5^1/_2$m	(9km)
55.	Bere Regis	$5^1/_2$m	(9km)
56.	Tarrant Gunville	6m	(10km)
57.	… and longer version	9m	($14^1/_2$km)
58.	Sixpenny Handley and Chase Woods	6m	($9^1/_2$km)
59.	Wimborne St Giles	6m	($9^1/_2$km)
60.	Chilcombe and Askerswell	6m	($9^1/_2$km)
61.	Lyme Regis and Charmouth	6m	($9^1/_2$km)
62.	Powerstock Common	6m	($9^1/_2$km)
63.	Wynford Eagle	6m	($9^1/_2$km)
64.	Sherborne	6m	(9km)
65.	Gussage All Saints	$6^1/_2$m	($10^1/_2$km)
66.	Farnham and Chettle	$6^1/_2$m	(10km)
67.	Ashmore and Tollard Royal	$6^1/_2$m	(10km)
68.	Milborne St Andrew and Tolpuddle	$6^1/_2$m	($10^1/_2$km)
69.	Milton Abbas	$6^1/_2$m	($10^1/_2$km)
70.	Spetisbury and the Rings	$6^1/_2$m	($10^1/_2$km)
71.	Morden and Lytchett Matravers	$6^1/_2$m	($10^1/_2$km)

PUBLISHER'S NOTE

We very much hope that you enjoy the routes presented in this book, which has been compiled with the aim of allowing you to explore the area in the best possible way – on foot.

We strongly recommend that you take the relevant map for the area, and for this reason we list the appropriate Ordnance Survey maps for each route. Whilst the details and descriptions given for each walk were accurate at time of writing, the countryside is constantly changing, and a map will be essential if, for any reason, you are unable to follow the given route. It is good practice to carry a map and use it so that you are always aware of your exact location.

We cannot be held responsible if some of the details in the route descriptions are found to be inaccurate, but should be grateful if walkers would advise us of any major alterations. Please note that whenever you are walking in the countryside you are on somebody else's land, and we must stress that you should *always* keep to established rights of way, and *never* cross fences, hedges or other boundaries unless there is a clear crossing point.

Remember the country code:

Enjoy the country and respect its life and work
Guard against all risk of fire
Fasten all gates
Keep dogs under close control
Keep to public footpaths across all farmland
Use gates and stiles to cross field boundaries
Leave all livestock, machinery and crops alone
Take your litter home
Help to keep all water clean
Protect wildlife, plants and trees
Make no unnecessary noise

The walks are listed by length – from approximately 1 to 12 miles – but the amount of time taken will depend on the fitness of the walkers and the time spent exploring any points of interest along the way. Nearly all the walks are circular and most offer recommendations for refreshments.

Good walking.

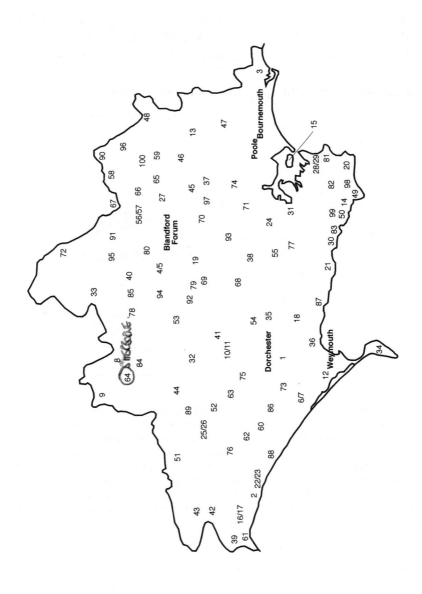

Walk 1   MAIDEN CASTLE $1^1/_2$m ($2^1/_2$km)

Maps: OS Sheets Landranger 194; Pathfinder 1332.

A fascinating walk around one of Britain's most important historical sites.

Start: At 664887, the car park at Maiden Castle.

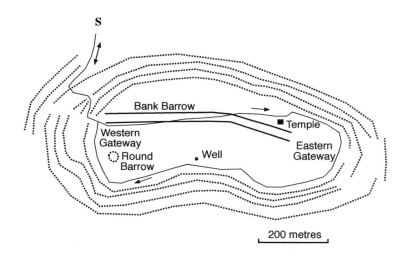

To reach the start, take the A354 southwards from the centre of Dorchester, heading towards Weymouth, and turn right at the edge of the town.

From the car park head south towards the ditches and ramparts of **Maiden Castle**, entering the site through the **western gateway** at its near end. Once inside the site, head eastwards, across the middle of the inner site, following the barely discernible **Bank Barrow** to reach, just to the left of a centre line, the remains of a **temple**. At the **eastern gateway**, bear right to follow the inner edge of the ramparts. Stay close to the inner rampart, passing a **well** and the damaged remains of a **round barrow** to regain the western gateway. Now reverse the route back to the car park.

POINTS OF INTEREST:

Maiden Castle – The first hill fort on the twin hillocks that form this site was built in Neolithic (New Stone Age) times, that fort ending at a now–inconspicuous bank about two-thirds of the way along Bank Barrow, at the 'col' between the two hillocks. Following its desertion by the Neolithic folk, the site lay quiet for 1000 years until it was re-occupied by Iron Age (Celtic) peoples. They expanded the site, building ditches and ramparts to enclose an area of 45 acres. There were multiple defences, the recent invention of the sling requiring the enemy to be kept well back, and even today after the erosion of centuries the ramparts and ditches are impressive. Within the defences a village of perhaps 4,000 people is believed to have grown up. The site's name derives from this Celtic village at 'Maidun', the big hill.

Western Gateway – Maiden Castle has one of the most elaborate gateways of any British hill fort, the jumble of ramparts being unravelled by the experts to record a clever maze of passageways that turned an attacker's unshielded right side to an array of defenders on top of the ramparts.

Bank Barrow – During the Neolithic occupation of the site the biggest long barrow in Britain was constructed there. Though barely discernible now, it is estimated that 100,000 tons of earth and rock were excavated to form the burial mound, which was 500 yards long, 20 yards wide and (probably) 10 feet high. Excavation has revealed the skeleton of a man, which can now be seen at Dorchester Museum.

Temple – After the Romans took the site they built a temple within it, perhaps to celebrate their victory. From the ramparts nearby there is a marvellous view of Dorchester which stands on the site of the Roman city of Durnovaria.

Eastern Gateway – Near the gateway Sir Mortimer Wheeler excavated the mass grave of the Celtic defenders of Maiden Castle who died when the Romans attacked in 43 AD. The site was one of the strongest in southern England and its overthrow imperative to the Roman invasion. One of the excavated skeletons, a Roman ballistae arrow lodged in its spine, can be seen at Dorchester Museum. Following the Roman victory, the site was occupied by the Celts for perhaps 20 years, and then abandoned.

Well – Within the hill fort there is both a well and a dew pond, though neither dates from the Iron Age occupation. What the Celts did for water is not known, though it is likely that they carried it in containers at a time of danger. In those days neither wars nor sieges lasted long so there would have been no need for a permanent supply.

Round Barrow – Despite there being no evidence of a Bronze Age occupation of Maiden Castle this burial mound was built at the site during that period.

REFRESHMENTS:
None at the site, but numerous possibilities in nearby Dorchester.

Walk 2   **GOLDEN CAP** $2^1/_2$m (4km)

Maps: OS Sheets Landranger 193; Pathfinder 1317.

A fine walk to the highest sea cliff in southern England.

Start: At 420918, the car park in Seatown.

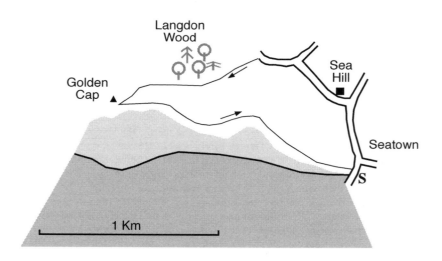

From the car park, walk back up the road towards Chideock for 600 yards, then turn left along a lane. Walk past 'Sea Hill' and on to a lane junction. Turn left again, into Pettycrate Lane and follow it westwards. The path follows the southern edge of the woods on **Langdon Hill**. Go through a gate and follow a hedge, to the left, to reach a path, also on the left, for **Golden Cap**. Follow this directly to the trig. point at the summit of the Cap. Close by is the **Antrim Memorial**.

After admiring the view, follow the Dorset Coastal Path eastwards. The cliff top on this section of the Coastal Path has suffered serious erosion, requiring the path to be diverted and for sections to be stepped to avoid further damage. Despite the intrusive nature of this work, the walking is superb, the view to the east – towards Eype Down and Thorncombe Beacon – holding the eye as a descent is made towards Seatown. Go

10

over a stile and turn right, as indicated by the Coastal Path sign, to return to **Seatown**. From the Anchor Inn, cross the footbridge to return to the start of the walk.

POINTS OF INTEREST:

Langdon Hill – The name Langdon is Saxon for 'long hill', making the addition of 'hill' superfluous. A local legend maintains that a clump of pines on the hill's northern end covers a mass grave of plague victims.

Golden Cap – At 191 metres (626 feet) Golden Cap is the highest sea cliff on the south coast of England. The name derives from a layer of golden sandstone which overlays the greyer rock of Wear Cliffs which fall from the Cap into the sea. This golden layer adds an extra leonine feature to the Cap when it is viewed from Lyme Regis. From the trig. point summit the view is exceptional, especially westwards to Lyme Regis and the coast beyond. The cliffs near Golden Cap have seen many landslides over the years – it is advisable to be cautious, and not to approach the cliff edge too closely.

Antrim Memorial – Much of the coastline near Golden Cap is owned by the National Trust, so it seems appropriate that its summit should have been chosen to raise a memorial stone to the Earl of Antrim who was Chairman of the Trust from 1966-1977.

Seatown – The picturesque village of Seatown is wedged into a narrow valley between the high cliffs of Golden Cap and Thorncombe Beacon. The thatched cottages and delightful inn look out over a shingle beach that was once popular with smugglers.

REFRESHMENTS:
The Anchor Inn, Seatown.

Walk 3   **HENGISTBURY HEAD**   3m (5km)

Maps: OS Sheets Landranger 195; Outdoor Leisure 22.

A short walk full of interest and with outstanding coastal views.

Start: At 164912, the café building at the Hengistbury Head eastern car park.

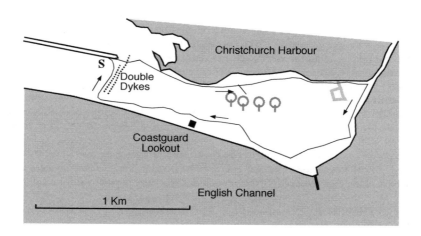

Hengistbury Head is an Ancient Monument and a Site of Special Scientific Interest. The area is owned by Bournemouth Corporation and managed by its Parks and Recreation Department. It is also maintained as a Nature Reserve. A visit to the Ranger's office at the east end of the café building is recommended before walking: here there are leaflets dealing with all areas of interest encountered on the Head - archaeology, geology, history and natural history. Hengistbury Head and its adjoining areas attract many thousands of visitors annually, so it is best to avoid weekends and holiday periods if you can.

From the café building, set off along the tarmac path through the **Double Dykes**. Shortly, on the right behind the maintenance area, the route passes a Bronze Age barrow. Next, Christchurch Harbour, the confluence of the Stour and Avon rivers, appears on the left. Soon after there is a wooded area on the right: this is a bird sanctuary (no entry) used by some migratory species.

Where the path bends right (by marker No. 12), branch left through some small trees on to the salt marches. Now keep to the main grassy path which leads towards a low mound covered with scrubby growth. Here a prickly 'tunnel' leads to the shore line. Cross a tidal inlet by bridge and rejoin the tarmac. Turn right and follow the line of beach huts to reach the cliff, at the end where a flight of shallow gravelly steps provides easy elevation.

The Head suffers badly from erosion and Nature's buffeting of the cliffs is evident. For their protection and that of visitors, restrictive fencing has been erected. Keep to the left-hand track, walking through a heathery stretch. On the right there is a large pool, once an ironstone quarry. Make for the coastguard hut and pause there to admire **the view** which has already commanded so much attention.

Now go downhill past the trig. point and fork left for the sea end of the Double Dykes. Turn right alongside them to return to the car park.

POINTS OF INTEREST:

Double Dykes – The most clearly visible sign of early habitation locally, the dykes were constructed about 2,000 years ago as the landward defence of the promontory settlement. Excavations have shown that the Head was inhabited 12,000 years ago and that there was a busy trading port here well before the Roman invasion.

The View – Look out to sea - the English Channel - and move clockwise. The first point of land is Durlston Head (12 miles away), then Swanage and Old Harry Rocks. Behind these are the Purbeck Hills. Studland beach and Poole Harbour come next, followed by the seafront and urban mass of Bournemouth. The ancient Christchurch Priory, the Harbour and the town of Christchurch are on the landside. The eroding cliffs between Barton and Milford lead to the stony bank of Henry VIII's Hurst Castle, guarding the entrance to the Solent. Finally, there is the Isle of Wight with the hump of Tennyson Down above the Needles and their lighthouse (8 miles away).

REFRESHMENTS:

There is a café by the car park, but for the largest selection of pubs, cafés and restaurants in the south of England, head west into Bournemouth.

Walks 4 & 5   OKEFORD HILL AND RINGMOOR   3m (5km) or 7m (11km)

Maps: OS Sheets Landranger 194; Pathfinder 1299 and 1300.

Excellent views, moderate gradients, with one steep hill on the shorter walk.

Start: At 813093, the car park on Okeford Hill.

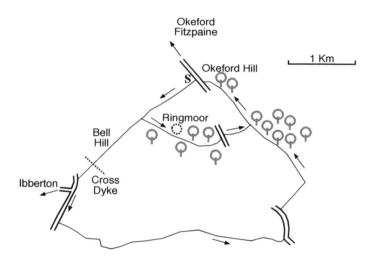

Go through the picnic area and over a stile. Turn right up the stony track, which soon passes two barns. There is a fine view north from here, with Melbury Down and Shaftesbury and the isolated Duncliffe Hill, all to the right of the expanse of Blackmore Vale.

For the shorter walk – turn left on to National Trust land through a gate by a pond. Bear right over the stile and walk close to a belt of trees. As the path begins to fall slightly, look left and you will see the **Ringmoor** earthworks. Continue down the slope past a gate and stile. The way is grassy through open woodland with a final steep drop to a road. Go through the gateway opposite and puff your way up to the top right corner of the field. Take the left-hand of two gateways and continue up the right side of the next field. At the top, turn left to rejoin the longer walk.

For the longer walk – visit Ringmoor, by all means, but return to the gate by the pond. The diversion is a round trip of just over $1/2$ mile. Continue on the main track over Bell Hill, eventually passing two radio masts. About 200 yards after the second one, you will pass the line of an ancient **cross dyke**. It is seen better on the left, just after a field gate. Descend to the road and turn left. Walk past the Ibberton turning (from here, it is a steep $1/2$ mile down to the Crown Inn, and a much steeper $1/2$ mile back again). Pass an ex-restaurant, then go left on to the grass. This is a favourite spot for motorists, with its view over Blackmore Vale.

Where a track crosses the grass, turn left along it. Follow this until you enter a field, then turn right downhill. Soon, turn left to walk above a deep, green valley. Keep to this track for a mile or more to reach the valley floor. Next, there is a cluster of farm buildings. Carry on past them to meet a road. Turn left and, after about 500 yards, turn right up a wide, stony track. Pass a barn and the track narrows, becoming grassy. When faced by a gate, turn left and walk between hedges up to a wood – well blessed with flowers in springtime. Keep to the left edge of the wood. After about $1/2$ mile, a gate leads to open grass. Go straight ahead, rejoining the course of the shorter walk.

Follow the bridleway across the shoulder of Turnworth Down. When you reach woods on the right, look back for a view of the Purbeck Hills. Turn left at the gate and walk down to the road and the car park.

POINTS OF INTEREST:
Ringmoor – The earthworks are the remains of Iron Age and Roman settlements. The area and the woodland below are administered by the National Trust.
Cross dyke – One of many to be seen on the downs of Wessex. They are believed to have been territorial boundaries.

REFRESHMENTS:
There is nothing directly available on these two walks but nearby are:
The Crown, Ibberton (*see* note in walk description).
The Royal Oak, Okeford Fitzpaine ($1^1/2$ miles north by road from the car park).

Maps: OS Sheets Landranger 194; Pathfinder 1331.
A famous village and an extension along a fascinating beach.
Start: At 561846, the car park at Chesil Beach.

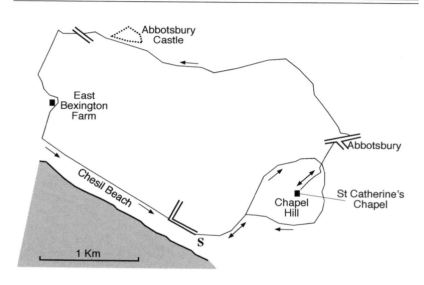

The car park is reached by turning left off the B3157, Abbotsbury to Bridport, road, going past the Tropical Gardens.

From the car park walk away from the road, along the beach to reach a stile on the left. Go over and follow a path, heading towards the prominent chapel on the hill ahead. Go over a stile and follow the track as it contours around Chapel Hill. Just beyond a stone barn on the right, go through a gate, also on the right, and climb up to **St Catherine's Chapel**. Reverse the route back down to the track and turn right. Bear left soon after to reach **Abbotsbury**.

The shorter route returns to the track after visiting the village, bearing right on a path that contours around the eastern side of Chapel Hill. Go over a stream and keep right. The path contours around the southern flank of the hill, though it is poorly defined in a couple of fields. Walk parallel to the Chesil Beach below, to reach the outward track. Now reverse the route back to the car park.

The longer route goes through Abbotsbury village: from Market Street, turn right into Back Street and, after 200 yards, go left on a track between thatched cottages. At a fork in the track bear left to go uphill between banks. Go through two gates, still rising steeply, and cross a field to another gate and signpost. Bear left, following the sign for 'Hill Fort', and continue uphill to reach a signpost at the top. Turn left along the ridge, following an alternative (inland) section of the Dorset Coastal Path. Go over a stile and continue, with superb views both along the coast and inland. Ignore a path heading down left to reach a lane. Cross and follow the path signed for West Bexington. Go over a stile and bear right to reach the hill fort of Abbotsbury Castle. Walk along the fort's southern rampart, then bear left to reach a gate on to a road.

Cross the road, go over a stile and follow a wall to a signpost. Turn left and follow the sign for Chesil Beach, going downhill on a path between trees and a fence. At the next signpost, go left to reach a fence and follow it to a stile. Go over and cross a field to another stile. Bear right, as indicated, crossing a field towards East Bexington Farm. Go through a gate, cross a field and go through another gate to reach a track around the left side of the farm. The track bears right, then goes ahead through a gate and across a field to reach the Coastal Path. Turn left along the Path or walk along Chesil Beach, a difficult beach to follow, but one that allows the walker to be close to the sea. Either the path or the beach will take the walker back to the start.

POINTS OF INTEREST:
St Catherine's Chapel – The chapel, built in the 15th century, has walls of such immense thickness that the inside seems tiny in comparison to the imposing outside. Its site made it a prominent landmark for sailors: it was known as the Seamen's Chapel, a name that also fitted well with the services held for the souls of drowned men.

Abbotsbury – This beautiful village is famous for its Swannery, situated on the Fleet, the brackish lagoon held back from the sea by Chesil Beach. Here there are several hundred swans drawn to the spot by an abundance of food in the Fleet. Within the village are ruins of an abbey founded in the 11th century by Orc, one of King Canute's house earls. There is also a fine 14th-century tithe barn, some 250 feet long, and a church (to St Nicholas) with a 15th-century painted glass window. The Tropical Gardens, on the way to the walk's car park start, were first planted by Lord Ilchester in 1760. The collections of azaleas, magnolias and camellias are excellent.

REFRESHMENTS:
There are several possibilities in Abbotsbury.

Walk 8   **SHERBORNE PARK**   3m (5km)

Maps: OS Sheets Landranger 183; Pathfinder 1280.
A fine walk through a Park steeped in history.
Start: At 670158, Hayden Church.

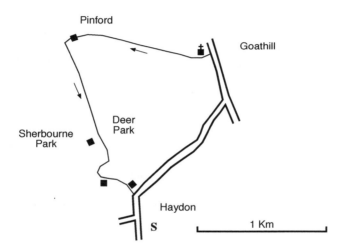

From the church go north, along the road, towards Goathill. After about a mile the road reaches a junction. Turn left towards Goathill, following the road to reach the hamlet's church, on the left. Turn left here, beside the church, on to a track signed for Pinford. Ignore a turn to the right, continuing between cottages and a farm to reach a gate at the end of the farmyard. Stay with the track, passing a pond, to the left, and continuing to a path junction. Go straight over and through a gate. Beyond this, bear left, away from the track, following the field edge to a gate on the left. Do not go through: instead, turn right and cross to another gate. Go through and turn left to reach two gates in quick succession.

Beyond the gates bear right to follow the field edge. Go around two sides of the field and continue along the third side to reach a gate set back on the right, just past a wooden building. Turn through this, walking past Pinford Farm. Just beyond the

18

farm house you will reach a stile on the left. Go over and head south to reach a gated bridge. Cross this and the field beyond to reach a gate in the wall. Beyond is the Deer Park of **Sherborne Park**. Maintain direction, crossing a track and passing a cottage, to the right, to reach a gate which marks the exit of the Deer Park. Go through and follow the fence on your left to reach a gate on to a track. Turn right along the track to reach a lane. Turn left and follow the lane, ignoring two turns to the right, to reach the Park Gates at a lodge. Go through and walk down to the road used on the outward journey. Now reverse the first few yards of that journey to regain the start.

POINTS OF INTEREST:
Sherborne Park – Sherborne is unusual in having two castles. The older one, to the north of the River Yeo, was built by Roger, the Norman Bishop of Salisbury. It was virtually destroyed during the Civil War and is now in the hands of English Heritage. One earlier owner of the castle tried to restore it, but gave up and built the new castle. He was Sir Walter Raleigh, one time favourite of Elizabeth I who was banished to Dorset after having had the audacity to marry her lady-in-waiting. When Raleigh left Sherborne for London and his execution he is said to have gazed at the Park he had helped create with his wife and sighed that it had all been his, but had been taken away from him. In fact, the Park our route traverses would barely be recognised by Raleigh, being another brilliant landscaping creation of Capability Brown.

REFRESHMENTS:
None on the route, but numerous possibilities in Sherborne.

Walk 9   **SANDFORD ORCAS**   3m (5km)

Maps: OS Sheets Landranger 183; Pathfinder 1260.

A fine walk near the border with Somerset.

Start: At 622211, Sandford Orcas Church.

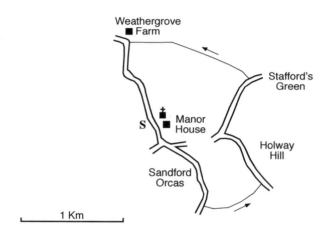

Head south along the village road, passing turnings to the right and to the left. Go past the Mitre Inn, to the right, to reach a signed footpath on the left. The path is almost immediately barred by a gate: go through and cross the field beyond to reach another gate in the far right-hand corner. Go through and bear right across a field to reach a gate. Go through this on to a track and turn left along it. Follow the track through a farm and on to a road. Turn left, following the road down Holway Hill.

      The road bends sharply left, after which there is a turning to the right signed for Carton Denham. Take this, following the road to Staffords Green. Here turn left, off the road, on to a lane that soon narrows and degenerates into a rough track. Follow the track to reach a road at a sharp bend close to Weathergrove Farm. Turn left and follow the road back to the church in **Sandford Orcas**.

POINTS OF INTEREST:

Sandford Orcas – The village is set close to an old ridgeway route used for centuries as a way of travelling between Maiden Castle and South Cadbury in Somerset. The name is of later origin and shows the interesting way in which some English place names have developed. Sandford is Saxon, and simply denotes a stream ford with a sandy bottom. Orcas derives from Oresculiz, the Norman family who took the manor after the 1066 invasion.

The village church is 15th century and houses a fine 13th century font. There is also a good alabaster monument to William Knoyle who died in 1607. An earlier member of the Knoyle family, Edward, was responsible for the construction of the excellent Manor House beside the church. The house, built of Ham Hill stone (as is the church), is Elizabethan, but on earlier foundations. The stone carving on the gatehouse is exquisite.

REFRESHMENTS:
The Mitre Inn, Sandford Orcas.

GODMANSTONE   3m (5km)
or 8m (13km)

Maps: OS Sheets Landranger 194; Pathfinder 1318.
Two fine Downland walks.
Start: At 666973, Godmanstone Church.

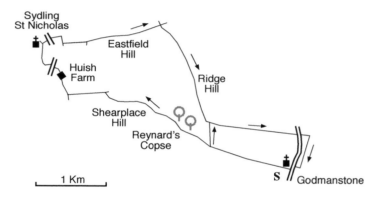

From the church, return to the A352, turn right for a few yards, then go right along a signed bridleway for Sydling St Nicholas. Follow the track as it climbs on to the top of the Down, passing a copse of trees on the right. At the Down top, there is a meeting of several tracks close to a clump of trees. Turn right along a ridge path (heading for the appropriately named Ridge Hill).

From here the shorter route follows the ridge path, then bears half-right to reach a hedge. Follow this, with it on your right-hand, to reach a signed metal gate. Here you rejoin the longer route.

The longer route also follows the ridge path, but very soon turns left to follow a fence (the fence is on your right-hand). Follow the fence to reach a track which descends the right side of a downland hollow to reach the edge of Reynard's Copse. Go through a gate and walk past a barn to reach a fence. Follow the fence – it is on your left-hand – until it turns sharply left. Here maintain direction along the track, climbing up the side of Shearplace Hill to reach a well-defined track. Turn left along this, descending into the Sydling Water valley. At a junction of tracks turn right that is, stay with the main track to reach Huish Farm. Here bear left on a track to a road. Turn right, but after about 50 yards, cross the road and turn left up an inclined bridleway. Follow the bridleway to its junction with a track. Turn right along the track to reach Court Farm and the church of **Sydling St Nicholas**. Turn right to reach the main village street. Cross into East Street and walk to its end. The Greyhound Inn is to the left from here, but the walk goes right on a signed bridleway for Large Bar Barn. Follow the track, which soon turns sharply left and heads steeply up Eastfield Hill. Where the track turns sharply right, go straight on through a gate, following the bridleway eastwards up the hill. Go through a gate to reach a track fork. Turn right, maintaining your easterly direction, beside a hedge. The bridleway crosses the flank of Eastfield Hill, then descends slightly into a hollow before rising up the hollow's far side. Go through two gates then bear half-left away from the hedge to reach the ridge crest and a crossing track. Turn right along the track. The track follows the ridge, going over Ridge Hill then descending slightly. Where the hedge to your left turns sharply left, go forward, passing a signed wooden gate to reach a signed gate where the shorter route is rejoined.

Turn through the metal gate, cross a field and go through another gate. Follow the hedge to your left, then go through it into the next field, turning to follow it on your right. Go through further gates to reach the A352. Cross, with great care, to reach a track down to the River Cerne. Go over a footbridge and turn right on a path along the riverbank. The path passes the Smith's Arms Inn, across the river, then reaches a footbridge. Go over this to reach the road **Godmanstone** and re-cross the A352, again with care, to return to the church.

POINTS OF INTEREST:

Sydling St Nicholas – The Court House beside the church is 18th century, but stands on the site of an earlier house of Sir Francis Walsingham, Secretary of State to Elizabeth I. The huge tithe barn – now roofed in iron rather than thatch – dates from Sir Francis' time. A beam is inscribed UW 1590 for his wife Ursula.

Godmanstone – The Smith's Arms is a single 17th-century thatched inn which claims to be the smallest in England, having one bar measuring 10 foot by 20 foot, with a very low ceiling. The story is told that Charles II stopped in the village in 1665 to have his horse re-shod and asked the village blacksmith for a drink while he waited. The blacksmith apologised, saying he could not give the King a drink as he had no licence to sell ale. The King promptly granted him one.

REFRESHMENTS:
The Smith's Arms Inn, Godmanstone.
The Greyhound Inn, Sydling St Nicholas.

Maps: OS Sheets Landranger 194; Pathfinder 1332.
A short introduction to The Fleet.
Start: At 634805, Fleet Church.

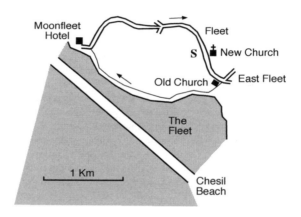

The **church** is reached by taking the Fleet road from the Chickerell roundabout on the B3157.

Walk back along the road to the sharp left bend. Turn right on a track, going through a gate to reach the **old church** and continuing to a track fork. Take the right-branch and walk to a T-junction of tracks. Turn left and follow a track towards **The Fleet**. At the water's edge, bear right through a gate and cross the field beyond, following the fence on your left to reach a stile. Go over, cross a footbridge and follow a path to reach a crossing path.

Turn right along the path, bearing right with it to follow the edge of the Fleet. The path reaches a T-junction close to a stile: go right and cross the stile. Now follow the woodland edge on your left to reach another stile. Go over and bear right across the field beyond to reach a crossing track. Turn right along the track to reach a gate on to a lane. To the left here is the Moonfleet Hotel. The walk turns right leaving the Dorset Coastal Path which has been followed to this point. Go along the lane to reach a cross-roads. Take the road ahead to return to the church.

POINTS OF INTEREST:

Church – This is the new Fleet church, built in 1829 at the expense of the village's vicar, John Gould. It has a magnificent chancel ceiling and a fine memorial to another John Gould, the vicar's son.

Old Church – On 23 November 1824 a ferocious storm (known locally as 'The Outrage') lifted the 90 ton sloop Ebenezer on to the crest of the Chesil Beach. But the storm also tore a hole in the Beach opposite Fleet village letting in waves that destroyed many of its cottages and all but destroyed the village church. Only the chancel remained and the vicar chose to build a new church rather than try restoring the old one. The village that was lost was the Moonfleet of J Meade Falkner's famous book on smugglers. In the church, now partially restored, is a plaque to Falkner and also several memorials to members of the Mohun family whose name gave the author the prefix for his village name. And just as the book says, there is a tunnel leading out from the church towards The Fleet, though whether it was ever used for smuggling is not known. On dark, stormy nights it is easy to imagine the ghost of Elzevir Block walking up the track from the water's edge.

The Fleet – Stretching for over 8 miles behind the bar of the Chesil Beach the Fleet is a Grade 1 SSSI (Site of Special Scientific Interest). Its waters, which become increasingly brackish as its connection with the sea (at the aptly named Small Mouth) is reached, being a text-book site for plants and animals in water of varying salinity. The waters support an impressive array of waders and wildfowl.

REFRESHMENTS:

The Moonfleet Hotel, on the route.

Maps: OS Sheets Landranger 195; Pathfinder 1301.
Easy walking on a heathland Nature Reserve.
Start: At 048037, White Sheet Hill car park.

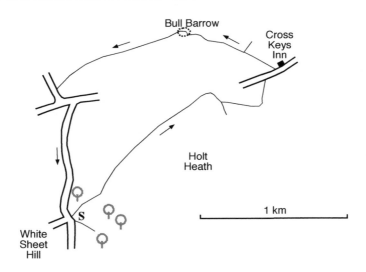

From the short approach lane face the car park, take the first track on the left (it is waymarked in blue) and head north-east. The path goes, at first, through young silver birches and then through pines, but soon reaches the open land of **Holt Heath.** Now, where vehicles have made a track swinging to the right, take a left fork, still following the blue waymarks and crossing the heath in the same north-easterly direction. Ignore all crossing paths, but definitely admire the blazing gorse or the rich purple heather in their seasons, until the path approaches a road. The track reaches a T-junction by a thick copse of young birches: turn right here, curving back towards the open heath. At a point where the track bends right again, turn left back towards the road and immediately take a tiny path on the right. This path soon leaves the heath, passing under trees and going behind a large white house. Where it meets a stony lane, turn left and go past houses to reach the road. Turn right and, in less than 100 yards, turn left up a track posted with signs entreating fishermen (!) to go slowly. A few more steps along the road from the turning will take you to the Cross Keys Inn, an excellent stop for refreshments.

Walk up the lane for about 400 yards, then keep straight on where it bends to the right. Pass through a belt of woodland to emerge on to another expanse of Holt Heath. Now head for the obvious height of **Bull Barrow**. From the barrow turn left along a broad track heading across the open heath, with Horton Tower (*see* Note to Walk 46) sitting prominently on the right-hand skyline. Continue straight ahead until a road is reached at one of the informative English Nature notice boards situated around the heath. Turn left along the road to reach a staggered cross-roads. Go across, taking the road signposted to Wimborne. Follow the road - following the roadside grass verge for much of the way - back to White Sheet Hill.

POINTS OF INTEREST:

Holt Heath – The heath is a National Nature Reserve administered by English Nature (Site Manager 0202 841026) for the National Trust which acquired the land in 1981 as part of the Kingston Lacy estate. It supports a wide variety of flora and fauna including many rare species. It was on Holt Heath – or, more accurately, at its edge – that the Duke of Monmouth was captured after the Battle of Sedgemoor. The battle took place on 6 July 1685, the Duke being captured on 8 July. He was taken to London and quickly sentenced to death. The Duke, a great believer in astrology, had once been told that in any year in which he survived St Swithin's Day he would outlive the year. St Swithin's Day is 15 July, and that was the day set for the execution. The Duke tried desperately to have the date moved back, even claiming at one stage that he had a cold in the head. But to no avail, and he failed to outlive St Swithin's Day.

Bull Barrow – The barrow is a Bronze Age burial mound.

REFRESHMENTS:

The Cross Keys Inn, Mannington.

Walk 14   **Kingston and Hounstout** $3^1/_2$m ($5^1/_2$km)
Maps: OS Sheets Landranger 195; Outdoor Leisure 15.
An easy walk with attractive views.
Start: At 954796, the car park at Kingston.

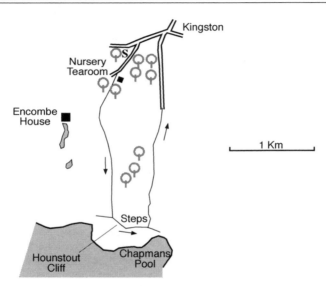

Leave from the rear of the car park and turn right at a signpost, 'Hounstout $1^1/_2$', going along an unmetalled road. The route passes through private woodland and, after another 500 yards, at the fork in the road, take the left-hand route, signposted for Hounstout. After a further 100 yards you will pass the Nursery Tearoom on the left. Continue for about a further 250 yards, then leave the woodland, going over a stile into open pasture land. The path beyond the stile follows a stone wall and ridge, with splendid views on the right into the Golden Bowl, with **Encombe House** below and Swyre Head behind it, to the right.

Continue along the ridge crossing the field to go over a stile into the next. The coast now comes gradually into view. Go over another stile and continue: there is now a magnificent coastal view stretching westward as far as Portland Bill. In the middle distance the Clavel Tower above Kimmeridge Bay can be seen. Go over the stile immediately before the cliff (there is a stone seat on the right) and turn left along the cliff edge coast path, which is stone waymarked for 'Chapman's Pool $1/2$ mile'. Almost immediately St Aldhelm's Head, with its former coastguard cottages and chapel, is seen. Then, as the steep descent of over 100 steps begins, Chapman's Pool comes into view.

At the bottom of the steps go over the stile on the left (the path continues to descend to **Chapman's Pool** which is closed to the public because of mud slides and cliff falls). Cross the large field beyond the stile to reach a gate. Go over a stream and, after 50 yards, turn left along a tarmac driveway which climbs up the valley towards Kingston. Go through a gate, or over a stile, after about $1/2$ mile, continuing up the road to go over the crest of the hill. Now descend into **Kingston**. At the church, turn left and walk up the road to return to the car park.

POINTS OF INTEREST:

Encombe House – The house was built in the 18th century and is situated in a beautiful valley known as the Golden Bowl.

Chapman's Pool – This cove is hollowed from the unstable clay and shale cliffs of Hounstout. There are a few fisherman's huts and a former lifeboat house, but the area is currently closed to the public because of the danger from mudslides and rock falls.

Kingston – The village has fine views of the Purbeck Hills and Corfe Castle. It once had two churches, but one of them became redundant and is now a private house. The remaining church, built by 3rd Earl of Eldon in the 1870s, is a fine example of the period and of the local stonemason's craft.

REFRESHMENTS:

The Scott Arms, Kingston.
The Nursery Tearoom, near Encombe.

Walk 15   BROWNSEA ISLAND   3¹/₂m (5¹/₂km)

Maps: OS Sheets Landranger 195; Outdoor Leisure 15.

An easy woodland walk with interesting wild life.

Start: At 032876, Brownsea Quay.

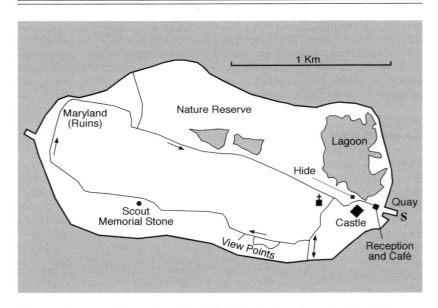

To reach the start of the walk, take the half-hourly ferry from the North Haven at Sandbanks (037871) or Poole Quay (012903). On disembarking go through the reception area and pay the landing fee (landing is free to National Trust members) and pick up the pamphlet and map of the **island**.

The walk follows the path, that leaves the reception area, to the right, by the walls of **Brownsea Castle** (to which there is no access). Pass a bird-viewing hide, on the right and continue along the gravel track. Turn left by the church (signposted 'To South Shore'). Here, on the grass to the left, is the open air theatre. Peacocks are often seen here. After about 100 yards, bear left (signposted 'To South Shore') and walk through the woodland to the shore. Here, and at subsequent viewpoints along the south side of the island, there are views across the water to the islands and wooded shore of Poole Harbour, with the Purbeck Hills behind.

Retrace your steps to a track on the left, and follow it around before bearing right at a signpost 'Cliff Walk and Viewpoints'. The path goes through woodland in which there are several opportunities to turn left to cleared areas where there are viewpoints. If any are visited, return to the main path. To the right of the path there are open grassy clearings in which deer can often be seen. Shortly, on the left by the path, is the Scout Memorial Stone.

Continue along the path, but at the next intersection take the path signposted 'To Maryland'. This soon bends to the right giving extensive views westward across Poole Harbour towards the Arne Peninsula and Wareham Channel. The path now heads north and descends, almost to the shore: Poole Quay can be seen about 1 mile away. On the right of the path are the ruins of the village of Maryland. At the next junction follow the path signposted 'To the Quay': this part of the walk is through the pine woodland and rhododendrons of the **Nature Reserve** that extends along the whole of the northern side of the island. Keep straight on, eventually passing the church before reaching the castle and quay.

POINTS OF INTEREST:

Island – Brownsea Island may be visited between April and September. Dogs are not permitted on the island. The island was given to the National Trust in 1962 in part payment of Mrs Florence Christie's death duties. In 1907 Lord Baden Powell held his first experimental camp for 20 boys here – the start of the Boy Scout movement.

Brownsea Castle – Henry VIII built the original block house by the quay. This was converted into a mock castle in the 18th century and is currently leased to the John Lewis Partnership. It is not open to the public.

Nature Reserve – About a third of the island is a Nature Reserve run by the Dorset Trust for Nature Conservation. The Trust organise tours of the Reserve which is open daily in July and August. The wildlife is of particular interest: there are red squirrels, Sika deer and lizards. Amongst the bird-life are peacocks, pheasants, cormorants, numerous species of wild duck, herons and various geese and seagulls.

REFRESHMENTS:

There is a National Trust café at the Quay.

Walks 16 & 17   **STONEBARROW HILL** $3^1/_2$m ($5^1/_2$km) or $5^1/_2$m (9km)

Maps: OS Sheets Landranger 193; Pathfinder 1316 and 1317.
Two glorious walks close to the Coastal Path.
Start: At 381933, the NT parking area on Stonebarrow Hill.

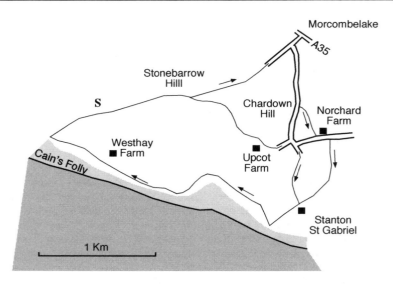

Continue along the track beyond the parking area, going through a gate to reach the National Trust Information Centre, housed in an old radar station. Continue along the track, which follows the ridge of Stonebarrow Hill. A track joins from the right and, just beyond and before a cattle grid and gate are reached, a path signed for Chardown Hill and St Gabriels goes off right.

The shorter route takes this path. Go through a gate, and bear left at a fork to reach a gate and stile. Continue through another gate, beyond which the path forks again. Take the right branch, bearing right and descending to reach a gate on to a track. Turn left and go through a gate to reach Upcot Farm. Follow the track, which goes between the farmhouse, on the right, and a cottage, on the left. Bear left at the farmyard along a track to a gate. Go through and continue, bearing left at a fork to reach a cross-roads of tracks (Pickaxe Cross). Turn right to follow the track signed for St Gabriels and Golden Cap. The track goes down to a gate marked as being private access to St Gabriel's Cottages. Go through this and continue, going over a bridge to reach **Stanton St Gabriels** where the longer route is rejoined.

The longer route continues along the main track towards **Morcombelake**. Just before the main A35 is reached another track goes off to the right. This is the route, but refreshments lie ahead, the Ship Inn being across the main road. Turn right to follow the track southwards passing, to the right, the **Holy Well**. Just beyond 'Coldharbour' go left on a path that crosses fields to Norchard Farm. Go to the right of the farm to reach a track. Turn left and, after a few yards, right on to a waymarked path that goes through woodland to reach Stanton St Gabriel and the shorter route.

Rejoin the Coastal Path, heading west along the top of a curious section of cliff. Numerous landslides have created an oddly tumbled, almost slumped, cliff which looks extremely unstable. The biggest of the landslides is Cain's Folly where the end of Stonebarrow Hill has collapsed into the sea. The route offers a fine view of the folly. At the head of the folly, turn right on a path that heads inland to reach the starting point.

POINTS OF INTEREST:

Stanton St Gabriel – In mediaeval times this was a thriving fishing community, but better road access to other small ports and the new road to the north of the village, together with the landslides for which this part of the coast is notorious, meant a gradual decline in the village's fortunes. By 1825 the village was virtually deserted. Today a few holiday cottages and the ruins of the old village church are all that remain. Local legend maintains that the church was once used as a smugglers' store, the Revenue men never thinking to look in such a holy place, even if it was ruinous.

Morcombelake – As Stanton St Gabriel declined, so the fortunes of Morcombelake improved, especially after the main road from Bridport to Charmouth, and on to Devon, had been opened. The church is dedicated to St Gabriel, a nice gesture as it replaced the coastal building. The village is famous for the production of Dorset Knobs, a special type of biscuit. The village bakery, which is open to visitors, makes these and Dorset Ginger biscuits, another local favourite.

Holy Well – The Well, sometimes known as St Wita's Well, is reputed to have miraculous curative properties, especially for eye problems. The saint of the name was killed by the Danes and is buried in the church at nearby Whitchurch Canonicorum.

REFRESHMENTS:
The Ship Inn, Morcambelake.

Walk 18   **WEST KNIGHTON** $3^1/_2$m ($5^1/_2$km)

Maps: OS Sheets Landranger 194; Pathfinder 1318.

A thought-provoking walk close to Dorchester.

Start: At 731876, West Knighton Church.

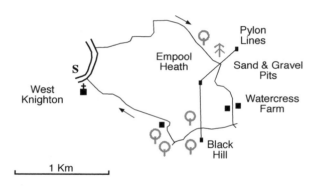

From the church go eastwards along the village street, turning left to head north, going downhill past the New Inn. At the bottom of the hill turn right along the road towards the Empool Pumping Station. Do not go to the pumping station: instead, go left, then right with the lane. The lane now drops towards a pit: go through a gate on the right and follow a track, passing a barn and heading towards the right-hand corner of a stand of woodland. To the right here is **Empool Heath**. At the wood corner there is a gate: go through and follow the wood's edge to reach a gate close to the pylon at its far corner. Go through the gate and turn right along a track. Where the track forks, beyond the pit, go right to reach a farm that specialises in growing watercress in the damp beds formed by streams draining the heathland down into the River Frome.

Go through the farm and walk to a track junction. Turn right and walk gently up Black Hill. Go under the power lines and through woodland. At the edge of another wood a track goes off to the right. Take this, following the wood edge to a stream. Cross the stream and turn right by a thatched cottage on to a path signed for West Knighton. Cross a ditch into a field and turn left along its hedge. Cross two fields then bear right to follow waymarkers across another field. On the far side go left along a track into a field. Now maintain direction, following further waymarkers to reach a stile. Go over on to a path and follow it to a lane. Turn right to walk between houses in **West Knighton** to reach a junction. Now turn right to return to the church.

POINTS OF INTEREST:

Empool Heath – Dorset is synonymous with heathland for, although heath is not unique to the county, the Hampshire Basin (covering parts of Dorset and Hampshire) has the finest heath in England. Heath forms on a base of sand or gravel that allows rapid percolation of water from the surface. This percolation removes nutrients, leaving a poor, acidic soil on which a surface layer of humus from recently decomposed plant life forms. The Dorset heathlands support the Dartford warbler, the smooth snake and a specific form of heather. Sadly, during this century some 85 per cent of Dorset's heathland has been destroyed by farming, building and the extraction of sand and gravel. Empool Heath was never the best section of heathland in the county, but the sand and gravel pits passed on the walk typify the problems of attempting to conserve ancient landscapes in the face of commercial pressures.

West Knighton – Although the village has expanded recently, its heart, around the fine 13th-century church, is still a delight.

REFRESHMENTS:

The New Inn, West Knighton.

Walk 19 WINTERBORNES STICKLAND AND CLENSTON 4m (6^1/$_2$km)
Maps: OS Sheets Landranger 194; Pathfinder 1300.
Extensive views. The only steep hill is downward.
Start: At 835047, the Shire Horse Inn, Winterborne Stickland.

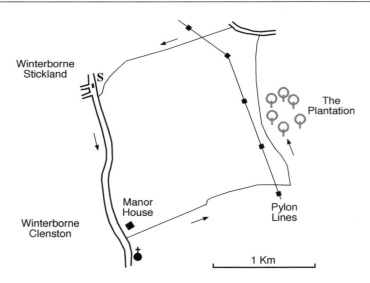

From the attractive village green, set off towards Winterborne Whitechurch with the
winter bourne itself running – if it is – on the right. Follow the road to **Winterborne
Clenston**. Turn left by the barns. The village church (1840) can be seen further on.
The track passes some farm buildings and then rises easily and straight – with one
little kink – to high open ground. Go under the power lines and through a small gate
from where there is an excellent view of east Dorset, with Charborough Tower on the
right and Badbury Rings ahead. Turn left. Go through a small steel gate and continue
along the edge of a field to reach a wood. Carry on past several large fallen beech trees.
Emerge from the wood and keep straight ahead, first on grass and then on tarmac.
When a road is reached, turn left and walk as far as a right bend. Here go left through
a gate and up the right side of a field.

With a gradual increase of height, the views get ever grander – the Purbeck Hills and the South Dorset Downs distantly, Turnworth Down to the north-west and Bulbarrow with the radio masts ahead. Cross a metalled track leading to the nearby Stickland mast and go steeply downhill. At the bottom, turn right for the village centre and the start of the walk.

POINTS OF INTEREST:

Winter bourne – In Dorset's porous chalk downland, a bourne (stream) will often run dry in its upper reaches when the water table drops, re-appearing after the heavier rainfall of winter. This River Winterborne (a tautological title) gives its name, going downstream, to the communities of Houghton, Stickland, Clenston, Whitechurch, Kingston, Muston, Anderson, Tomson and Zelston. There is another string of Winterbo(u)rnes to the south of Dorchester.

Winterborne Clenston – The fine Tudor manor house (built around 1470) is the ancestral home of the de Winterborne family. It is not open for general viewing. The barns are of similar antiquity: the tiled one has an impressive hammer beam roof believed to have been brought from Milton Abbey (*see* Note to Walk 92).

REFRESHMENTS:
The Shire Horse Inn, Winterborne Stickland.

Walk 20   SWANAGE AND DURLSTON HEAD   4m (6¹/₂km)

Maps: OS Sheets Landranger 195; Outdoor Leisure 15.

A coastal and pastoral walk with fine views.

Start: At 028788, Swanage Bus and Railway Station.

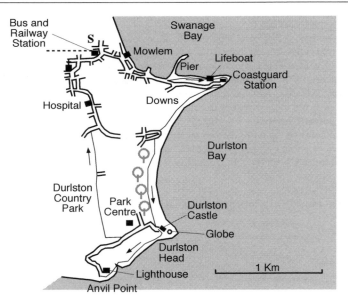

From the bus and railway station go down the main street (Station Road) to the Mowlem Theatre and sea front. Turn right along the front, passing the Stone Quay and Pier, then ascend the hill and, after 30 yards, turn left at a signpost for 'Lifeboat and Peveril Point via Beach Path'. (You can go straight on for 500 yards – signposted 'Peveril Point and Lifeboat' – if the tide is well in). The beach path goes past Swanage Sailing Club, the Wellington Clock Tower, some fisherman's huts, the **RNLI Station** and the former coastguard cottages to reach the coastguard station. Now follow the Victorian Trail waymark, climbing to the Down by the cliffs of Durlston Bay. Turn near the top at the stone seats and admire the view over Swanage Bay. On a clear day Ballard Down and the cliffs to Old Harry Rocks, Bournemouth, Hengistbury Head, the Needles Lighthouse, the Isle of Wight and St Catherine's Lighthouse can be seen.

At the top of the Down go through a gate and turn left into Belle Vue Road. Immediately after passing a block of flats on the left, go down the steps into Durlston Country Park. Go over a footbridge, keep to the left at the next intersection and proceed up the wooded way for 600 yards. At the crest, descend, passing **Durlston Castle** on the left. (A detour can be made to the right here, going through the car park to the **Durlston Country Park Centre**). Beyond the Castle, follow the bollarded descent, noting the London origin of the bollards, to reach a viewing point for the sea birds on the cliffs. Turn left, and after 50 yards examine the large Portland Stone **Globe**. Return to the viewing point and continue along the cliff edge path to Tilly Whim Caves (now closed as they are unsafe). The path now descends steeply, and then ascends along the seaward side of **Anvil Point Lighthouse**. Turn inland at this point, following a road back up the hill. Immediately the top is reached, turn left (westward) along a path. After about 100 yards, immediately beyond a copse, turn right on a path which heads northwards alongside a field and then descends to South Barn, passing it on the right. Climb up to go between houses to reach a road (Russell Avenue). Turn right, and at its end go left down Bon Accord Road. Go past the hospital, turn a corner and take the second road on the right (Townsend Road) into the High Street. Cross, keep to the right of St Mary's Parish Church and turn right into Kings Road. The combined bus and railway station is about 150 yards along the road, on the left.

POINTS OF INTEREST:
RNLI Station – The boathouse is open daily so that the lifeboat, the *Robert Charles Brown*, can be viewed.
Durlston Castle – This Victorian 'folly' was built in 1880 by George Burt. It is now an inn, restaurant and café.
Durlston Country Park Centre – The Centre was built by Dorset County Council on the site of the original radar research station which was transferred to Malvern at the beginning of the Second World War. The Centre houses exhibitions on local flora, bird life and quarrying.
Globe – The 40-ton Great Globe was built in sections at John Mowlem's Greenwich yard in 1887 and assembled on site.
Anvil Point Lighthouse – Built in 1881, the lighthouse is now automated and, therefore, closed to the public.

REFRESHMENTS:
The Durlston Castle Inn, on the route.
There are also numerous inns and cafés in Swanage.

Walk 21 LULWORTH COVE AND MUPE BAY 4m (6¹/₂km)

Maps: OS Sheets Landranger 194; Outdoor Leisure 15.

A short strenuous walk with fine views.

Start: At 831806, West Lulworth First School and Youth Hostel, or at 822801, Lulworth Cove car park.

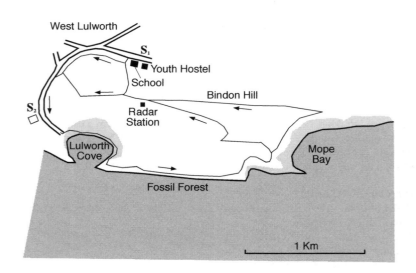

Warning: This walk is over the MOD Lulworth Range. This is generally open at weekends and throughout August. However, it is imperative that walkers check to ensure the range is open and that, for their own safety, they keep between the yellow markers.

From the school, go down the road, passing the school playing field and going over the stile adjacent to it. After 50 yards turn right over a stile signposted 'W Lulworth'. The path beyond is joined shortly by another, from the right, from the car park of the Castle Inn: continue for about 400 yards, then take the path stone waymarked for 'Sunnyside'. At a T-junction turn right, and then go left immediately above the main road and continue along it.

Pass (or leave) the Cove car park and go down the road to **Lulworth Cove** itself. At the bottom of the road turn left and walk along the shoreline. Go past waymarked steps, taking the path at the end of the Cove and following it as it climbs up the steep cliff. At the top (where there is a viewpoint) turn left along the seaward edge of the cliffs. Go through the steel gate into the **Lulworth Range** and turn right to the cliff edge to examine the **Fossil Forest** beneath the cliff. Continue along the cliff edge, keeping between the yellow markers, and go past a small Radar Station. Gradually a spectacular view of high white cliffs develops.

At Mupe Bay, the energetic can take the stone waymarker for 'Coast Path Kimmeridge $4^3/4$'. Go over a stile and climb the very, very steep cliff path. At the top turn left at the stone signpost for 'Radar Hill $^1/2$ and Lulworth 1' and go over a stile on to Bindon Hill ridge. The walk to the Radar Station gives marvellous views inland and along the coast. The less energetic should turn left at Mupe Bay, following the stone waymarker for 'Bindon and Radar Hill $^3/4$'. When the track reaches the crest, turn right – stone waymarker for Radar Cross – and follow the track up to the Radar Station where the routes meet. Now follow the stone waymarker for 'Lulworth Cove' and shortly leave the Range through the gate.

Turn right at the stone waymarker for 'Youth Hostel $^1/2$' and descend, following the edge of the Range. Go over a stile into a field, at the bottom of which are the school and Youth Hostel. For the main car park follow the stone signpost for 'West Lulworth $^3/4$', going down the hill to the road and turning left to reach it.

POINTS OF INTEREST:

Lulworth Cove – This small, circular natural harbour was formed when the sea breached the soft limestone cliffs. Formerly a haunt of smugglers, it is now a very popular tourist spot.

Lulworth Range – The range is part of an extensive tract of land from Kimmeridge Bay to Lulworth Cove and inland to West Holme which is used by the army for the gunnery training of tank and armoured vehicle crews. It was acquired in 1943 by the then War Department.

Fossil Forest – The forest is formed from the fossilised stumps of trees which grew millions of years ago.

REFRESHMENTS:
The Castle Inn, West Lulworth.
There are also possibilities at Lulworth Cove.

Walks 22 & 23   **THORNCOMBE BEACON**   4m (6^1/$_2$km)
or 7m (11km)

Maps: OS Sheets Landranger 193; Pathfinder 1317.
Two fine expeditions by Coastal Path and high Down.
Start: At 420918, the car park in Seatown.

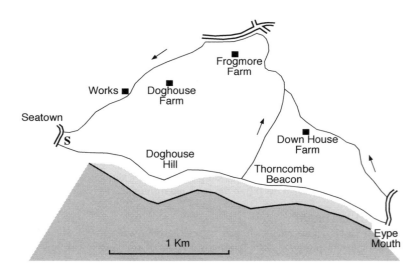

From the car park follow the signed Coastal Path eastwards. The Path goes over several stiles, then climb steeply up Ridge Cliff. Close to the top the Coastal Path leaves the cliff edge, heading inland slightly to cross the flank of the curiously named Doghouse Hill. The top of the hill can be reached, but the views are much better from the summit of nearby Thorncombe Beacon. Follow the path around Doghouse Hill, then head up to the summit of **Thorncombe Beacon**.

From the Beacon's summit the shorter route heads inland, going between a pair of tumuli, ancient burial mounds. Go past Down House Farm – one field away to the right – bearing left along a field edge to reach the longer route on Eype Down.

The longer route follows the Coastal Path eastwards from Thorncombe Beacon, descending into a delightful grass bowl, then rising briefly to follow a rickety fence along the **cliff edge**. The Coastal Path now drops straightforwardly into Eype Mouth where there is a café, and a car park which could be used as an alternative start. From the car park follow the road inland, leaving it through a gate to the left at a National Trust signpost for Down House Farm. Follow the track beyond, going to the left of some bungalows and over a stile. Follow the hedge to the right, then go right through a signed gate. Follow the path beyond, going uphill and through two gates to reach a track. Turn left and walk to Down House Farm. There, turn right along a signed track. The track goes through scattered woodland before emerging on to **Eype Down** and rejoining the shorter walk.

The route now follows a path through the gorse and bracken on Eype Down. Keep ahead at a path junction, heading almost due north to reach the main A35 at a cottage. Turn left at the cottage, following a path that runs parallel to the main road, crossing the drive to Frogmore Farm before swinging left to leave the road. Cross fields to reach the drive to Doghouse Farm, to the left. Go straight over, continuing along the path to reach a kissing gate at a point where a path comes in from the right. Go through and bear left around the edge of a sewage plant. Go along a concrete track, cross a stream and turn left through a kissing gate at a sign for Seatown. Cross a field and a track to reach another kissing gate. Go through, cross a footbridge and follow a concrete track to a lane (Mill Lane). Turn left and follow the lane to a road. Turn left to return to the start.

POINTS OF INTEREST:
Thorncombe Beacon – At 155 metres (508 feet) the Beacon is second only to Golden Gap in height, but is a better viewpoint. On clear days, to the west the Cobb at Lyme Regis can be seen, with the Devon coast beyond. To the east the long line of Chesil Beach, ending at Portland Bill, can be seen. The cliffs below the Beacon are also interesting, the shrubby growth being home to many birds.
Cliff edge – The cliff here is one of the finest sections of the Coastal Path for plant life, the heathery vegetation being interspersed with clumps of sea pink, mallow and bedstraw. The edge is also popular with kestrels. The fence keeps the walker from the unstable cliff edge, though the fence itself seems almost as unstable.
Eype Down – This is an excellent wild piece of commonland, the paths forcing a way through tall ferns and gorse.

REFRESHMENTS:
The Anchor Inn, Seatown.

Walk 24   **WAREHAM FOREST**   4m (6¹/₂km)

Maps: OS Sheets Landranger 195; Outdoor Leisure 15.

A walk from one of Dorset's most famous inns.

Start: At 903896, the Silent Woman Inn.

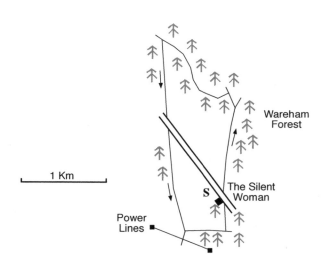

The **Silent Woman Inn** lies beside the road that cuts through **Wareham Forest** from the A351 just north of Wareham to the A35 (Dorchester to Poole/Bournemouth) road, meeting the latter to the east of Bere Regis.

From the inn walk north-west, away from Wareham, for a few yards, then cross the road to reach a forest road. At a Y-junction just a few yards into the trees, bear left. Now ignore turnings to the right, following the forest road as it goes along the edge of the forest, with fields to the left. Bear left at the next junction, where the road is joined by a wider one. Next, turn left on a forest road heading westward. This new road crosses a once marshy area, using a footbridge at one point. Go over the first crossing track, but turn left at the next to follow a signed bridleway southward.

Walk past a forest watchtower to reach a gate. Go through and continue southward. Go over a bridge, then continue between a caravan park, to your left, and woodland, to your right. The bridleway reaches a road: go straight over and continue along it, still heading southward. The bridleway is marked by blue arrows: follow these through the forest to reach a clearing. Here bear left towards the corner of a second caravan park. There turn right, following further blue arrows beside a fence (keeping it on your left-hand side).

Ahead now high-voltage electricity cables cross from left to right. Just before reaching these you will reach a signed footpath going off to the left. Take this, returning to the forest. At a crossing track, turn left and follow the track to a road. Turn left and follow the road back to the start.

POINTS OF INTEREST:

The Silent Woman Inn – The inn is called the Angel in Thomas Hardy's Return of the Native, perhaps a reference to one version of the story of how it acquired its name. That version has its origin in an early Christian saint beheaded by Viking invaders. The more gruesome, but also more plausible version, has it that the inn was used as a base by a gang of smugglers who, fearing that the landlady, a well-known gossip, would reveal their identities, cut her tongue out to ensure her silence.

Wareham Forest – The forest crossed by the walk is owned by the Morden Estate, being leased to the Forestry Commission. Apart from the bridleway the paths are permissive and should be followed without diversion. The lucky walker may see Sika deer as there has been a herd in the area for many years.

REFRESHMENTS:
The Silent Woman Inn, on the route.

Walks 25 & 26   **MAPPERTON AND HOOKE PARK**   4m (6^1/$_2$km)
or 6^1/$_2$m (10^1/$_2$km)

Maps: OS Sheets Landranger 194; Pathfinder 1317 and 1298.
Short walks in the Lost Valley.
Start: At 524004, the northern edge of Hooke Park.

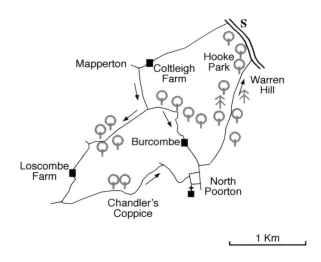

To reach the start point, take the road southward from Hooke to reach a T-junction and turn right. The road soon reaches the wooden edge of Hooke Park. Here parking is possible on the right-hand side of the road.

Just beyond the northern edge of the woodland there is a gate on the left. Go through and follow the bridleway beyond all the way to Coltleigh Farm. Maintain direction along the farm drive for about 100 yards, then turn left down a green lane. The farm drive continues to **Mapperton**, the detour being very worthwhile. However, our route takes the lane as it descends steeply down into a fine combe to reach a T-junction with a bridleway close to a small lake.

From here the shorter route turns left, following the bridleway to reach the edge of the Hooke Park woodland. The bridleway now bears right to follow the wood edge then turns sharp right and downhill into the combe. Near the valley bottom the bridleway bears left to cross a stream. Continue to reach Burcombe taking the lane that leads south-east from there to rejoin the longer route at the northern end of North Poorton.

The longer route turns right along the bridleway which threads its way along the beautiful combe to reach a track junction. Turn left, passing a ruin and fording a stream, and following the stream's left bank to reach Loscombe Farm. Now take the farm drive and follow it into the hamlet of Loscombe. When the main village street is reached, at a T-junction, turn left and, soon after, go right on a signed path that heads eastward, following a stream. Cross the stream at a waymarker and follow the path uphill to reach the southern edge of Chandler's Coppice. Now follow the southern edge as it bends right, then left with the hill contour, where the wood stops, maintain direction, passing a barn to reach a lane. Turn right and follow the lane to a T-junction in **North Poorton**. Turn right and follow the road past the church to reach another T-junction. Turn left and head north on a lane, passing through the last of the village. Where this lane bears distinctly left the shorter route is rejoined.

Go east across rough ground, soon reaching a blue waymarker and a gate. Go through and follow the bridleway beyond into a field. Bear left towards the woodland of Hooke Park, reaching, and following, a hedge to a gate. Go through and walk along the wood edge (with it on your right-hand) to reach a footbridge. Go over and follow the bridleway through the forest, ignoring all side turnings as you rise up towards the top of Warren Hill. The bridleway does not visit the hill's top, going around the western side and on to a road. Turn left to return to the start.

POINTS OF INTEREST:

Mapperton – The beautiful Manor House is open to visitors who will enjoy the splendid panelling and ceilings. Equally interesting is the Posy Tree, an old oak named for the posies of flowers left here as protection by the very few locals who survived the outbreak of Black Death in 1660.

North Poorton – The church here was built by John Hicks a Dorchester architect whose one-time apprentice was Thomas Hardy.

REFRESHMENTS:

None on the route, but available at Toller Porcorum, to the east, and Powerstock, just to the south of North Poorton.

Walk 27   TARRANT MONKTON   4¹/₂m (7km)

Walk 27   **TARRANT MONKTON** $4^1/_2$m (7km)

Maps: OS Sheets Landranger 195; Pathfinder 1300.
Mainly farm track walking, with some gentle slopes.
Start: At 944088, Tarrant Monkton church.

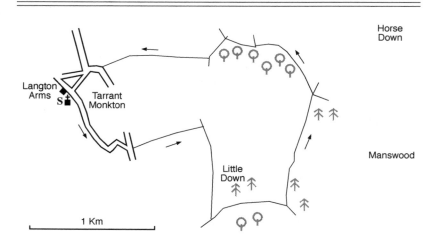

Turn right from the church forecourt and walk along the road through the village.
Bend left at a farm and cross the River Tarrant. At a junction, take the track on the
right across the road. The track rises gradually for nearly $1/_2$ mile. Turn right at the
top of the slope, passing a vehicle barrier, and walk along a ridgeway. From here, the
broad fields sweep down to the **Tarrant Valley**.

Continue to a junction, and there turn back to the left. Ignore the first turning
right, following the main track as it bends right to pass between conifers and coppice.
A field opens on the left: at a T-junction, turn left on to a wide track with a larch
plantation now on the right. The track rises and swings slightly as it moves into open
land. In autumn and winter, pheasants abound here and deer and hare may also be
seen. On the slight descent that follows, there is another larch plantation on the right,
rich with resinous scent. Turn left at a cross-roads on to another stony track. Now, with

woodland on the left, keep on to reach a reservoir on the right at the top of the slope. Here turn left, go past a vehicle barrier and bear right downhill. The route enters the much-thatched Tarrant Monkton over the 300-year-old packhorse bridge: another 200 yards of walking will bring you back to the church and the Langton Arms.

POINTS OF INTEREST:

Tarrant Valley – Meandering peacefully through the soft beauty of its valley, the Tarrant is remarkable for its baptism of no less than eight villages in the course of 10 miles. Going downstream, it claims Gunville, Hinton, Launceston, Monkton, Rawston and Rushton before Keyneston and Crawford break the alphabetical progression.

REFRESHMENTS:
The Langton Arms, Tarrant Monkton.

Walks 28 & 29 AGGLESTONE AND BALLARD DOWN 4¹/₂m (7km)
or 6¹/₄m (10km)
Maps: OS Sheets Landranger 195; Outdoor Leisure 15.
A hilly heath and downland walk with panoramic views.
Start: At 036828, the Middle Beach car park, Studland.

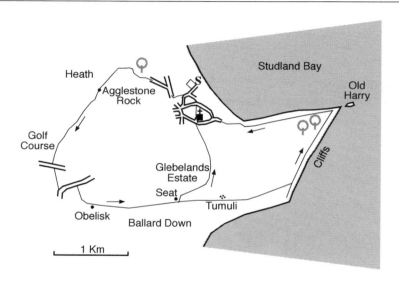

Turn right from the National Trust car park, passing Beach Cottage, to the right. At the Trust's winter car park take the signed footpath on the right. Follow a path and stream to the main road. Turn right, cross the road and after 50 yards take the left-hand path into Wadmore Lane. Pass a cottage and farm and take a path signed 'Agglestone Rock'. Go over a footbridge and through woodland to reach open heath (a National Nature Reserve). Turn left at a signpost. **Agglestone Rock** can now be seen ahead: continue to it, pausing there to enjoy the view of Poole Harbour, Poole Bay and Bournemouth.

Climb steadily across Godlingston Heath and after the path levels, turn half-right at a stone waymark (Studland Road ¹/₂ mile). Walk along the edge of the golf course to reach a gate to a road at Dean Hill. Turn left for 30 yards, then go over a stile on the right and cut across the golf course, heading for 7th green (but keeping it on the left) and a wood. Descend through the wood, go over a stile and aim for the stile in bottom right corner of a field to reach a road. Turn left and walk along the grass verge for 150 yards, then take a footpath on the right and climb to the **obelisk** on Ballard Down. Go through the gate at the obelisk and a further gate on the crest of the Down. Proceed for about $^1/_2$ mile, enjoying the panoramic views of Poole Harbour, Poole Bay, Bournemouth, Hengistbury Head, Isle of Wight and Swanage.

For the shorter route: ignore the first footpath on the left, continuing to a path junction. Here, go through the gate on the left immediately passing the 'Rest and be Thankful' stone seat, dating from 1852. Descend, going through a gate at the Glebeland's Estate and continuing down to Manor Farm. Here, at the cross-roads (note the modern replica of an earlier Saxon Cross) take Church Road, signposted 'Church Only'. Continue into the churchyard, passing the west end of the church and keeping straight on to reach a minor road. Turn right and, after 50 yards, turn left passing the Manor House Hotel to reach the starting car park.

For the longer route: keep straight on at the path junction. Go through a gate, pass a tumuli and, after about $^1/_2$ mile, descend steeply and veer left to reach the cliff edge. Carry on until **Old Harry Rocks** are reached. The path now turns sharply left, following the cliff. After about $^3/_4$ mile follow a stone waymark to a road. Turn right, passing the Bankes Arms Hotel and, later, the Manor House Hotel to return to the starting car park.

POINTS OF INTEREST:
Agglestone Rock – This large ironstone rock weighs about 400 tons and stands 17 feet high.
Obelisk – This was erected by George Burt in the 19th century to commemorate the establishment of the local water supply. The needle was demolished in 1941 as it was thought to be a useful land mark for the enemy and re-erected after the war.
Old Harry Rocks – The larger chalk pinnacle is Old Harry, the smaller one Old Harry's Wife, much smaller since a ferocious storm in 1896.

REFRESHMENTS:
The Manor House Hotel, Studland.
The Bankes Arms Hotel, Studland.
There is a café at Middle Beach and a tea rooms in Studland.

Walk 30   FLOWERS BARROW AND TYNEHAM $4^1/_2$m (7km)

Maps: OS Sheets Landranger 194; Outdoor Leisure 15.

A varied hilly walk, initially on a heath ridge, with a sharp descent to the sea and returning via a deserted village and climb.

Start: At 888812, the Whiteway Hill car park.

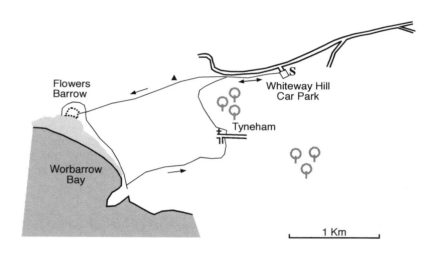

Warning: This walk is over the MOD Lulworth Range. This is generally open at weekends and throughout August. However, it is imperative that walkers check to ensure the range is open and that, for their own safety, they keep between the yellow markers.

Leave the car park through the gate on the west side and follow the stone waymarker for 'Flowers Barrow 1'. This is a well defined path between yellow markers. As the walk progresses there are splendid views, to the left, of Tyneham village and Worbarrow Bay and inland, to the right, over the tank training ground to Lulworth Castle. After about $^1/_2$ mile there is a junction of paths: keep straight on, passing the trig. point summit of Whiteway Hill on the right. Continue to **Flowers Barrow**. Go to the seat on top of the Barrow and admire the view, which extends from St Aldhelm's Head, to the east, to Portland, to the west.

Leave the Barrow by following the stone waymarker for 'Coast Path Worbarrow Bay $^3/_4$'. The path initially descends steeply (with optional steps), then goes over stiles to reach a footbridge by the shore at Worbarrow Bay. Cross, and after about 30 yards take the lane that rises from the beach. Continue up the valley for $^2/_3$ mile to reach **Tyneham**. Turn left through the car park into the village. Immediately before the church, go over the stile on the right, and follow the stone waymarker for 'Whiteway car park 1'. Follow the track uphill, and at the crest turn right, following a stone waymarker for 'Whiteway car park $^1/_2$'. Follow this path back to the starting point of the walk.

POINTS OF INTEREST:

Flowers Barrow – This is the inappropriate name given to the Iron Age hill fort, with a circular ditch and earth bank, on top of Ring's Hill. The hill is one of the last breeding places of the rare Lulworth skipper butterfly, and is also the home of a ghostly Roman army. The army is usually only heard, as the tramping of feet across the grass, but in the late 17th century was seen by over 100 people. Convinced that a foreign army had landed at the coast and was marching inland the locals sent word to Wareham and the local militia was quickly organised. They hurried to the hill, but their supposed enemy had disappeared. From the hill fort there are splendid views along the coast.

Tyneham – This village and the land surrounding it was commandeered by the War Department in 1943 as a training ground for Allied Forces. The village has never been returned to its rightful owners. The village church and schoolroom are open to the public: there is an exhibition in the church and the schoolroom is set out with 1920s desks on which there are exhibits of pupils work.

Because the land around the village has not been worked, the flora and fauna has been preserved from the ravages of modern farming methods.

REFRESHMENTS:

None on the walk, but available in nearby East Lulworth.

Walk 31   **WAREHAM AND THE RIVER FROME** $4^1/_2$m (7km)
Maps: OS Sheets Landranger 195; Outdoor Leisure 15.
An estuary walk by river bank and marsh.
Start: At 924874, the Howards Lane 'long stay' car park,
Wareham.

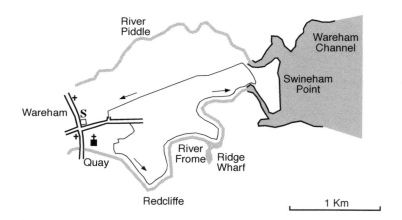

On this walk it is advisable to wear Wellington Boots during or after wet weather.

Turn left out of the car park and go left again into South Street. At the traffic lights,
turn left and go down East Street, passing the market and auction rooms on the right.
The road breaches the old town walls and becomes Best Wall Road: after passing a
cul-de-sac turn right on a path signposted 'Footpath to River Bank'. After 50 yards,
go through a gate and after a further 25 yards go right over a stile. Continue over
another stile and two footbridges, then turn left to reach the riverbank. The path,
which can be considerably overgrown with long grass, goes along the north bank
of the **River Frome**, offering views of the collection of yachts moored along the
far bank.

After about $^1/_2$ mile Redcliffe (on the other bankside) is reached and after a further $^1/_2$ mile Red Wharf is similarly passed. The river meanders for a further $^1/_2$ mile, after which a left turn is taken over a sluice. Immediately beyond, turn right to rejoin the riverbank, following the waymarkers. The path leaves the river and follows the outer boundaries of a field. At this point there is an extensive view over the salt marshes of Swineham Point and Poole Harbour. The going for the next $^3/_4$ mile is marshy, but improves after you go over a footbridge. Beyond the bridge, turn right, ignoring the sign pointing ahead. After 25 yards the path turns sharply to the left: go with it, then cross a stile and follow the path beyond as it skirts a plantation.

Go over a stile into a wooded lane. Cross the road to the ECC Quarry and continue along it. At the bend climb up on to the **Wareham** town wall and walk to the left. Go past the first exit off the wall, but take the second on the right. This is East Street: follow it to the traffic lights, turn right and go right again to return to the Howards Lane car park.

POINTS OF INTEREST:

River Frome – The river was used to transport goods, clay and coal to and from Wareham, making it an important port until silting caused a reduction in trade. Today the river is used extensively for mooring yachts.

Wareham – This attractive town is Saxon in origin, King Alfred having fortified it after capturing it from the Danes. The massive earthen walls he erected still survive in places. After a disastrous fire in 1762 the town was rebuilt in elegant Georgian red-brick style. The small church of St Martin, mainly Saxon, but with Norman additions and one of the oldest churches in the county, at the north end of the town has an effigy of T E Lawrence (Lawrence of Arabia). Holy Trinity Church near the quay is now an art gallery. The principle church, of Lady St Mary, was substantially rebuilt in 1842, it has retained many interesting medieval artefacts. The quay is popular with yachtsmen and with the Old Granary is very picturesque.

REFRESHMENTS:

There are numerous opportunities in Wareham.

Walk 32   CERNE ABBAS   4¹/₂m (7km)

Maps: OS Sheets Landranger 194; Pathfinder 1299.

A walk past Britain's most intriguing hill figure.

Start: At 663015, the Kettle Bridge picnic area/car park, Cerne Abbas.

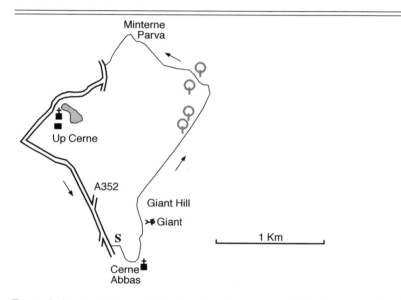

To reach the start, take the A352 from Sherborne towards Dorchester, turning left off it for Cerne Abbas. Now go first left, signed 'Village Centre' to reach the picnic area/car park.

From the car park go back to the road and turn left towards a bridge. Do not go over: instead, turn right on to a path beside the River Cerne. At a fork, go left, over a footbridge, and follow a path to Abbey Street, **Cerne Abbas**. Turn left, towards the abby ruins, to reach a pond. Keep it to your right, then go right through a gate elegantly set in an archway. Beyond is a cemetery. Go diagonally across this, exiting through a similar gate. Maintain direction (with the abbey ruins to your left) across a field to reach a stile. Go over on to the clear path up Giant Hill. Follow the path beside the fence which protects the Giant, to the right.

When the fence ends, maintain direction at first, then bear slightly right over the ridge to reach a waymarker post. Stay with the gorse bushes to reach a stile. Go over and bear half-left across a field, aiming for the right edge of a copse where there is a waymarker post. Maintain direction across the next field to reach a gate on the left. If you go as far as the road you have gone too far! Go through the gate and bear slightly right across the field beyond to reach another gate. Beyond this, ignore a path along the field edge: instead, go downhill through trees to reach a gate in a hedge. Go through this and cross the field beyond to reach a track. Follow this track to a gate, beyond which it bears right to pass a house (on the left). Continue to reach a crossing track.

Turn left, following the track to a lane through Minterne Parva, and continuing along this to a road. Turn left and follow the road to a turning, on the left, for **Up Cerne**. Take this road, passing the church and manor house and continuing to a sharp left-hand bend. Go with the road, following it to reach the main A352. Turn right, with care, soon reaching the Giant View lay-by, the best viewing point of the **Cerne Abbas Giant**. Now bear left, then turn left, to return to the start.

POINTS OF INTEREST:
Cerne Abbas – A Benedictine monastery was founded here in the 10th century, though little of it now remains. The best of the remnants is the elegant 15th-century three-storied gateway. Elsewhere, any walk through this beautiful village is worthwhile.
Up Cerne – This delightful hamlet has a 15th century church and a 16th century manor house.
Cerne Abbas Giant – This robustly male chalk-cut figure is 180 feet tall. Its origins are not well understood: it could be pre-Roman, Roman (a figure of Hercules?) or early post-Roman. The experts agree it is a fertility figure – but surely that could not have been in doubt?

REFRESHMENTS:
The Royal Oak Inn, Cerne Abbas.

Walk 33   **MARNHULL** $4^1/_2$m (7km)
Maps: OS Sheets Landranger 183; Pathfinder 1280.
A walk from Tess' village.
Start: At 781188, Marnhull Church.

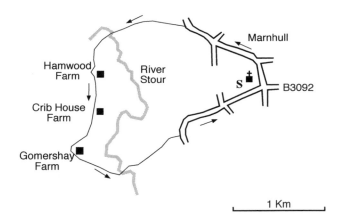

From the church walk down to the B3092. Turn left along it, but almost immediately
go left again to follow the road through **Marnhull**. Stay with the road, going around a
sharp left bend and continuing to reach the **Blackmoor Vale Inn**. Continue along the
road for a few yards, then bear left into Ham Lane, following it to its end. Go through
the gate ahead into a field. Follow its left hedge to reach a gate, also on the left. Go
through, turn right and cross to another gate. Go through this to reach a bridge over
the River Stour. Walk beside the river to reach a stile. Go over this and another soon
after, then turn left and cross a field towards Hamwood Farm.

   Just before the farm there is a waymarked gate on the right: go through, then
turn left to go through another. Cross the farmyard and go through a gate into a field.
Cross to reach a pair of stiles. Go over these and cross a field to another stile. Cross
and head towards the right-hand side of Crib House Farm. Go over a stile and bear left

to a gate beside a barn. Go through and follow a track to the left, passing the farm to reach a signed gate. Now follow further waymarkers, going over a stile and heading for the right-hand side of Gomershay Farm. Go through a gate on the right, then bear left on to a track. Follow the track past the farmhouse, then cross a footbridge over a tributary stream of the River Stour.

Now cross a field to reach the River Stour, crossing it on a footbridge. Bear half-right to reach a gate and walk ahead to reach another on to a lane. Go ahead, along the lane, bearing right to reach a road. Turn left along the road, staying with it as it reaches Marnhull and returns to the **Church**.

POINTS OF INTEREST:

Marnhull – This qualifies as the most well-spread village in Dorset, its houses being built around a square of roads that suggest a size out of all proportion to the number of inhabitants. In *Tess of the d'Urbervilles*, Thomas Hardy renamed the village Marlott. Here Tess was born. One cottage in the village is now called Tess' Cottage. The Crown Inn is probably the model for Hardy's *Pure Drop Inn*. Nash Court, at the north-eastern end of the village was once owned by Catherine Parr, the sixth, and last, wife of Henry VIII.

Blackmoor Vale Inn – In *Tess*, this is *Rollivers*. The inn was built as farm cottages in the 16th century, but later knocked into one to become a brewery and inn. Today the brewery has closed, but the fine old inn remains.

Church – This beautiful church dates from the 15th century and has a fine altar tomb from that time, decorated with alabaster effigies. Look, too, for the epitaph to Ruth and John Warren, pipe smokers.

REFRESHMENTS:
The Blackmoor Vale Inn, Marnhull.
The Crown Inn, Marnhull.

Walk 34   PORTLAND BILL   4¹/₂m (7km)

Maps: OS Sheets Landranger 194; Pathfinder 1343.
The most distinctive cliff walk in Dorset.
Start: At 676683, the Portland Bill car park.

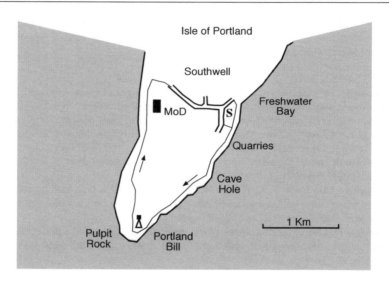

This route goes around the tip of the **Isle of Portland.** Although not technically an island, being joined to the mainland by a causeway formed by the southern extremity of Chesil Beach, Portland has a distinct island feel. To reach the start take the A354 from Weymouth. The road crosses the causeway and rises through Fortuneswell, passing an excellent **viewpoint** before continuing to Easton. Now follow signs for Portland Bill.

From the car park near the **lighthouse**, go south to the cliff edge, then turn right to follow the cliff past **Pulpit Rock**. Go around the fence of an Admiralty complex and take the path that heads back towards the cliff edge. From here the view across the water to Chesil Beach and, on clear days, further along the coast towards Golden Cap, is magnificent.

Go past another Admiralty complex, and continue for another 300 yards or so to reach a distinct track heading inland. Turn right along this to reach a road. Follow the road, ignoring all side turnings, to reach the Eight Bells Inn, Southwell. Turn right. Now take the first turning left along a **quarry** road which leads back to the cliff edge. Turn right along the cliff path, passing several old sea quarries and **Cave Hole**, and continuing back to the lighthouse on Portland Bill. Now reverse the few steps back to the start.

POINTS OF INTEREST:
Isle of Portland – Often described as the 'Gibraltar of Dorset', Portland was called the *Isle of Slingers* by Thomas Hardy as, anciently, its inhabitants were good with the slingshot. From very early times, the value of the natural harbour between the Isle and Weymouth was recognised. The construction of the breakwaters created one of the world's largest harbours, a strategic base for the Royal Navy. The Isle's remoteness also made it an obvious place for a prison.
Viewpoint – The Isle's cliffs are not high, but at its centre it rises to over 400 feet. The viewpoint makes the most of this height, offering a superb view over Chesil Beach, Portland Harbour and Weymouth.
Lighthouse – The first lighthouse at the Bill was built in 1720, offering ships protection from the treacherous Portland Race.
Pulpit Rock – This is a huge outcrop of the famous Portland stone.
Quarry – Like the Isle of Purbeck, Portland is famous for its hard building stone. Wren used it to face St Paul's Cathedral.
Cave Hole – This is a natural, not quarried, sea cave with a blow-hole in its roof.

REFRESHMENTS:
The Eight Bells Inn, Southwell.

Walk 35   STINSFORD   4¹/₂m (7km)

Maps: OS Sheets Landranger 194; Pathfinder 1318.
Hardy's Cottage and three fine hamlets.
Start: At 724923, the car park at Higher Bockhampton.

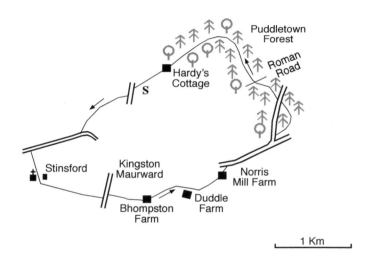

The start point is reached from the A35 a couple of miles north-east of Dorchester.

From the car park go back to the road and turn left. After a few yards go right along a track towards the farm at Higher Bockhampton. Go through a gate to the left of the last farm building into a field and follow its right edge to another gate. Go through and cross the field beyond to its bottom right-hand corner where a gate gives access to a track. Turn left along the track to reach a road. Turn right along the road to reach a signed track for Stinsford Church and School, to the left. Follow the track past **Stinsford Church**, continuing along it when it becomes a tree-lined path to reach a T-junction. Turn left along another tree-lined path that takes a causeway across boggy ground close to the River Frome.

The path ends at a road. Turn left towards the village of **Lower Bockhampton** and Kingston Maurward, and turn first right towards a farm. Go between the farm buildings, but when the track bears right go through the waymarked gate ahead. Cross a field to a stile and go over into the next field. Follow its right edge and go over another stile, continuing to reach a track at Bhompston Farm. Cross this, go over a stile and cross the field beyond to reach another stile. Go over and cross a track for Duddle Farm. Cross a field and go over a stile to reach a track that bears half-left to Norris Mill Farm. Go through the farm to reach a road.

Turn right along the road, passing Duck Dairy House and then turning first left on a road heading northwards towards Puddletown. After just a few yards go right on a bridleway into the forest. Follow the bridleway to reach a driveway. Turn left and, very shortly after, go left again at a track fork. Where the track forks again go left and walk to a road. Go straight across and follow the forest track to a fork. Take the right branch and follow it to its intersection with an old Roman road. Cross the old road and follow the main track, ignoring turnings to the right and left to reach a junction with a larger track. Cross this and continue for 100 yards to a path fork. Bear left here, and again at another fork about 100 yards further on, to reach a junction of six tracks. Take the second track to the left and follow the blue waymarker arrow, to reach Hardy's Cottage. Now follow the well-known track south-westwards back to the start.

POINTS OF INTEREST:

Stinsford Church – St Michael's was the church of the Hardy family, Thomas' father and grandfather singing in the church choir. Hardy's ashes lie in Poets' Corner, Westminster Abbey, but his heart was buried here. Here, too, lie the bodies of Hardy's two wives and several members of his family.

Lower Bockhampton – In Hardy's novels this is Lower Millstock. It was here that Fancy Day taught at the school in *Under the Greenwood Tree*, a school that the young Thomas actually attended.

Hardy's Cottage – The small two-storey thatched cottage was built by Thomas Hardy's grandfather in 1800. Here, on 2 June 1840, Thomas was born. Here, too, he wrote *Under the Greenwood Tree* and *Far from the Madding Crowd*, two of his best known books.

REFRESHMENTS:

None on the route, so bring your own and make use of the picnic area, or take a short drive to Dorchester where there are numerous possibilities.

Walk 36   **WHITE HORSE HILL** $4^1/_2$m (7km)

Maps: OS Sheets Landranger 194; Pathfinder 1332.

Fine views and a famous chalk figure.

Start: At 724830, Osmington Church.

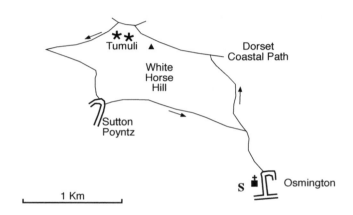

Head north from the church, but do not turn with the road, going, instead, along the lane that continues northward towards **White Horse Hill**. This section of the walk is along the inland variation of the Dorset Coastal Path and is well signed. Follow the track beyond a gate to the top of the hill. There the track joins a ridge track: turn left along this, going through a gate. The track continues in fine style, going through another gate and passing, to the left, the trig. point summit of the hill.

Beyond a gate the track joins another. Turn left – still following the Coastal Path – walking past a pair of **tumuli** to reach a gate on the left, by a ruin. Go through and bear right with the track to reach a gate. Go through and start out across the field beyond. When you reach a line of telegraph poles, turn left with them to reach a track. Turn left along this, descending to reach a gate, on the right. Go through and follow a track into **Sutton Poyntz**, going through two gates to reach the village road. Turn left to a T-junction. The Springhead Inn is to the right here, but the route goes left, turning right almost immediately to reach a signed gate. Go through this and cross several fields, linked by gates. After crossing another field a curious wooden crossing point is reached in a hedge. Use this to gain another field and bear right across this to reach a gate. Go through and walk ahead to cross a small stream. Now continue towards the gate ahead. Go through this to rejoin the outward route in **Osmington**. Turn right to return to the church.

POINTS OF INTEREST:
White Horse Hill – The figure for which the hill is named is the only chalk-cut horse in Britain to have a rider. The figure is huge, covering almost an acre, and is usually said to be of George III and to have been cut to commemorate his visit to Weymouth in 1808. This is, however, disputed, another story having it cut (at around the same time) by members of the Royal Engineers awaiting transit to the Napoleonic Wars. In *The Trumpet Major*, Thomas Hardy offers a third version, claiming the figure was cut to commemorate the Battle of Trafalgar.
Tumuli – These are Bronze Age round barrows.
Sutton Poyntz – The village beneath White Horse Hill is the *Overcombe* of Hardy's *The Trumpet Major*. With its mill-pond and thatched cottages it is charming.
Osmington – Osmington is a straggling, but elegant, village with a church that suffered a little at the hands of Victorian restorers. Only the 15th-century tower is truly original. The manor house beside the church was the home of the Warham family whose memorials grace the church walls. One of the family was an Archbishop of Canterbury in the 15th century.

REFRESHMENTS:
The Springhead Inn, Sutton Poyntz.
The Sunray Inn, Osmington.

Maps: OS Sheets Landranger 195; Pathfinder 1300.

Grassy tracks in Dorset's pleasant land, but with one short, steepish rise.

Start: At 933047, the True Lovers' Knot Inn, Tarrant Keyneston.

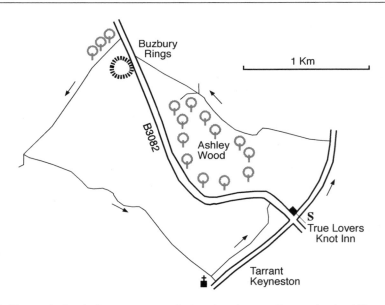

Parking at the Inn is for customers only, but there is a small stony lay-by 100 yards north-east along Tarrant valley road.

Take the road up the Tarrant valley for $^{1}/_{2}$ mile – there is not usually much traffic – then turn left up a grassy path signposted Buzbury Rings. The path rises easily, bending left and right, then continuing with Ashley Wood on the left. Where a metalled track comes in from the right, bear left and then take the right-hand of two tracks. At this point, there is a good view of Badbury Rings (*see* Note to Walk 45) behind you.

The golf course landscape on the left is soon joined by more golf on the right, but the path continues undaunted, drawing closer to the road (the B3082) and finally reaching it at a gate with a footpath sign. Visible across the road are the earthworks of **Buzbury Rings**. At the road, be careful as it is very busy. Turn right and walk for 200 yards, then cross the road and take a bridleway alongside a wood. Now, on the left, there is a more peaceful view of Buzbury Rings.

The bridleway leads to a gate. Go through this and then a smaller gate on the right. Keep to the left of the field beyond and stay to the left in the next field. A short lane now leads to a third field. Just before a line of overhead wires, turn left over a double stile and head half-left to a nearby angle of the hedgerow where sharp eyes will detect a faded yellow waymarker on a post. Follow the right side of the field and then take a track to some farm buildings. Circle these on the left and go steeply to the top right corner of a field. Climb the barred stile and go left over the ridge, passing two odd yews, before joining a track. Follow the track which slopes gradually down to **Tarrant Keyneston**. The church can be seen to the right.

As you reach habitation - some white cottages with small gabled windows - turn left on to a footpath on the near side of them. Go over stiles and along a narrow passageway to reach a long, thin field. Keep to the right and walk up to a stile in the corner. Go over and at the end of the next field a gateway leads to the noisy B3082. Turn right, with great care, to reach the starting inn which is about 200 yards down the hill.

POINTS OF INTEREST:

Buzbury Rings – The rings are an Iron Age earthwork. The foundations of dwellings have been found within the inner rampart.

Tarrant Keyneston – The village name derives from the de Kahaines family, Lords of the Manor in the 12th and 13th centuries. The church, All Saints, mostly dates from 1852 but has a 15th-century tower.

REFRESHMENTS:

The True Lovers' Knot, Tarrant Keyneston.

Walk 38   **BERE REGIS AND TURNERS PUDDLE**   5m (8km)
Maps: OS Sheets Landranger 194; Outdoor Leisure 15.
Over the hill to the Piddle valley and back by a heathland ridge.
Start: At 846948, the car park in the centre of Bere Regis – follow
the signs.

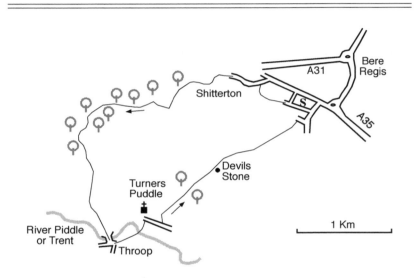

Leave the **Bere Regis** car park by the approach road and turn left. At the bottom, cross
the road and the cut grass and turn right along the delightful streamside boardwalk.
Continue on gravel where this ends, ignoring a footbridge to the left. On reaching a
road, turn left over the bridge into and through **Shitterton** with its many charming
cottages. Beyond the dwellings, go up a private road marked with a blue bridleway
arrow. This rises by a series of square turns, the traffic noise soon yielding to the
peace of the slopes above.

Turn right on a crossing track. With farm buildings on the right, go left through
a small steel gate. Cross the field, keeping to the right to find a small wooden gate in
a damp corner. Join the main woodland track ahead. This runs along a ridge at first,
and then wriggles a bit, going generally to the left and eventually downhill. Free from

trees, the track passes a chalkpit and goes on through fields. Turn left at a junction, then right 100 yards further on. This path by the river meadows crosses the River Piddle at Throop.

Here, turn left on the road and immediately left again up a farm track. Re-cross the river by footbridge or ford (twice) to reach Turners Puddle and the now redundant 16th-century church. Turn right, then left at the end of the farm. Bend left with the bridleway and turn right through a gate. The track rises slowly between hedges and enters a wood. In the open again, the way becomes steeper as it crosses slopes of heather, gorse and bracken – part of Hardy's Egdon Heath.

Go straight over at a gravel crossing and, after only 20 yards, the **Devil's Stone** is on the right. Continue on this path, now grass and level, and cross another track. Ignore a small left fork and carry on ahead. The path narrows as it drops down to a grassless clearing under trees. Go half-left on a sheltered path between fields. Level at first, this then freewheels down beside a cemetery. Walk through housing to the main road and turn left to cross the Bere stream – note the watercress farm. Beyond Elder Road, turn left to visit the churchyard. Paths from there lead to the car park or to Bere's traffic-calmed main street and the inns.

POINTS OF INTEREST:

Bere Regis – The town had royal associations in medieval times. Queen Elfrida, of murderous fame at Corfe Castle, once lived here and King John is thought to have had a hunting lodge locally, though it has never been found. Simon de Montfort, founder of the English parliament, also lived here. The largely 15th-century church of St John has the tombs of the Turberville family.

Shitterton – Although shown on most maps as Sitterton (or even Shutterton), the Bere Regis Parish Council has always formally used an official spelling with an 'h', as it was of old. Official village and road signs are also spelt in this manner. In the Domesday Book (1086), the area was recorded as Scetre, Old English for dung or manure. Local opinion is divided.

Devil's Stone – A sarsen stone with Bronze Age tumuli nearby.

REFRESHMENTS:
The Drax Arms, Bere Regis.
The Royal Oak, Bere Regis.

Maps: OS Sheets Landranger 193; Pathfinder 1316.
A fine walk through beautiful country.
Start: At 324933, Uplyme Village Hall.

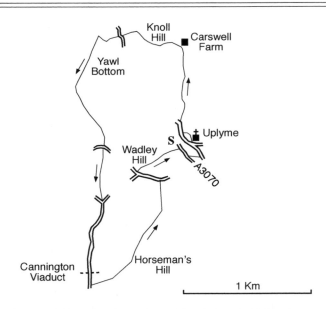

Head south, towards Lyme Regis, turning left just before the Talbot Arms on a path to
Church Street. Turn left and walk to the church. Go through the churchyard and the
new cemetery beyond to reach a gate. Go through and turn right along the lane. Just
before Carswell Farm, go left on to a signed footpath. Go over two stiles then head
uphill to a third. Go over and follow a fence around the southern flank of Knoll Hill.
Go over a stile and cross a field to a gate. The track beyond leads to the main road.
Cross, with care, and go steeply down Cathole Lane.

    At the junction with another lane a signed path, to the left, heads south. Take
this path along Yawl Bottom, a delightful valley. Go past Cathole Farm, to the right,
and a lake, to the left, to reach woodland. A track joins from the right: follow this,
passing several houses and continuing to a road (Woodhouse Lane). Go straight over

and cross a stile. Follow the path beyond across a field, looking to the left to see the top of Golden Cap. Go through a gate and diagonally left to reach a stile. Go over on to a road at a Y-junction. Go straight down the road ahead (heading southwards) to reach **Cannington Viaduct**. Continue along the road, leaving it by going through a gate on the left just before Loomhouse.

Follow the path beyond the gate to reach a lane (Cuckoo Lane) at Horseman's Hill Cottages. Now follow the lane along the base of Horseman's Hill to reach a stile, on the left, just before a red-brick house. Go over and take the right-hand of two paths. Cross the old railway line (the line that once ran over Cannington Viaduct) and bear half-right to reach a stile at the corner of a field. Go over and turn left to follow a hedge. Now go left to reach a stile, go over and cross a stream. Several old railway sleepers now help the walker over a section of marshy ground. Go down the right-hand side of a field to reach a hedged path. Follow the path to a road. Turn left, up the road, to reach a signed path on the right. Follow a hedge at first, then go half-right to reach **Uplyme** cricket pitch. From there it is a short step back to the village hall.

POINTS OF INTEREST:

Cannington Viaduct – The viaduct was built in 1903 and carried the London and South-Western Railway to Lyme Regis. The elegant bridge is 206 feet long and 93 feet high and was one of the first large scale concrete structures to have been built in Britain.

Uplyme – This delightful village stands on the River Lime, a river which names both it and nearby Lyme Regis. The church dates from the early 13th century and houses a fine early 17th-century Jacobean pulpit.

REFRESHMENTS:
The Talbot Arms, Uplyme.

Walk 40   **FIDDLEFORD MILL**   5m (8km)

Maps: OS Sheets Landranger 183 and 194; Pathfinder 1280 and 1281.

A walk through fine Dorset meadowland.

Start: At 790142, the car park at the old station, Sturminster Newton.

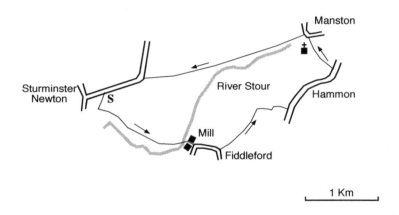

Leave the car park through the entrance you used to enter it, cross the road and follow the alley straight ahead. At the alley's end turn left along **Penny Street**. Towards the bottom, on the left, there is a farmyard: continue for about 25 yards, then turn left along a laurel-edged track signed for Fiddleford. Cross the field at the track's end to reach a gate. Go through and cross the field beyond, following the left hedge to reach a stile on to a footbridge. Cross the bridge into another field, and go across this, heading for the right-hand side of some farm buildings. Cross a footbridge at the field's corner and turn right, crossing a field to reach another footbridge. This bridge crosses the River Stour to **Fiddleford Mill**.

Go between buildings on to a metalled road. Follow the road to its junction with a more major road. Go ahead, soon reaching the first buildings of Fiddleford village. The main village is around the right-hand bend ahead, but the walk goes left at the bend, taking a bridleway signed for Hammoon. Follow the left edge of a field at first, but where this turns away go half-left across the field to reach a gate in the far hedge. Go through and cross the **old railway** to reach another field. Turn right and cross the field corner to a hedge gap. Follow the right edge of the field beyond to reach a gate. Turn right through the gate and follow the left edge of the field beyond to reach a gate on to a track. Follow the track, soon bearing right, through a gate, to follow the left edge of a field to reach a road. Turn left and walk to the village of Hammoon.

Go through the village, then cross the River Stour and continue for about 50 yards to reach a signed path (for Manston) on the left. Cross two fields, aiming to the right of trees on the far side of the second to reach a gate on to a road. Turn left, go over a bridge and immediately go left along a track signed for Sturminster Newton. Follow the track to a field and cross to the River Stour. Now follow the river bank, but where the river bears away left, go straight ahead. Go through a gate and across a field, moving closer to the river again as it bears back right. The ground ahead starts to rise: walk to the far, right-hand corner of a field and cross a footbridge. Turn left and walk uphill, heading for the left end of some buildings to reach another footbridge. Cross this and the field beyond to reach a road (the B3091). Turn left along the road, following it back to Sturminster Newton, turning left to rejoin the car park.

POINTS OF INTEREST:

Penny Street – William Barnes, Dorset's most famous dialect poet, was a pupil of the Street's Boys' School and later worked as a solicitor's clerk in Vine House, opposite the school.

Fiddleford Mill – The mill house is part of a manor house built in the 14th century for William Latimer, Sheriff of Somerset and Dorset. It is now in the hands of English Heritage who have carefully restored the superb open timbered roof and upper living room, each of which is the best of its kind in the county. The mill catwalk offers a great view of the machinery used to control water flow. Be sure, too, to read the 16th century inscription beseeching the miller to be an honourable man rather then one who might 'disgrace his vest'.

Old Railway – The track carried the Somerset and Dorset Railway, built in 1876, but closed down in 1967.

REFRESHMENTS:

There are numerous possibilities in Sturminster Newton.

Walk 41   **THE PIDDLE VALLEY**   5m (8km)

Maps: OS Sheets Landranger 194; Pathfinder 1318.

A walk that follows Dorset's most historically important river.

Start: At 712982, the European Inn.

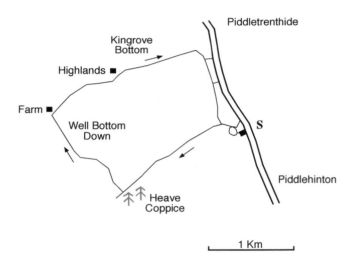

Go down the lane at the side of the **inn**, going away from the B3143. Go right, behind the inn, then left at a junction on to a lane that ends at a bridleway. Turn left here – the continuation of the bridleway to the right is the walk's return route. Follow the bridleway uphill, going over the hill's crest and descending towards the corner of Heave Coppice. There, a collection of three gates is reached. Go through the first of these – it is to the right – and follow the edge of the field beyond to reach another gate. Go through and follow the track beyond. The track crosses two fields on Well Bottom Down, going through a gate between them. Cross the second field to reach a gate on to a farm drive. Turn right.

The route has been climbing steadily since leaving Heave Coppice: continue uphill along the drive. Soon, the ground levels out: go past Highlands, aptly named for its position at the edge of College Down, above Kingrove Bottom, then start a descent into the Piddle Valley. As the valley is reached the track bears right. Go with it, but where it bears left to cross the **River Piddle**, go straight on through a gate. Cross the field beyond to a gate on to a track. Do not go left: instead, walk ahead, ignoring another turn to the left to reach a junction of tracks. Turn left here to reach the outward route. Now reverse the outward route back to the inn.

POINTS OF INTEREST:

The European Inn – It is claimed that this is the only inn in Britain to have the name. The origin is not certain, but it is certainly older than the Common Market, so that is not the reason. Some claim it is named for the European wars of the 19th centuries, but that seems a very odd idea.

River Piddle – The river's name is much more certain than the inn's. It derives from the Saxon for a clear stream, the lavatorial connotations of the name being added many centuries later. There was a time when some valley dwellers tried to alter the name to Puddle, claiming Tolpuddle (of martyr fame) as proof of its correctness. Thankfully the move was resisted. The nearest valley village to the walk, Piddletrenthide has ancestors of Thomas Hardy's d'Urbervilles buried in its churchyard.

REFRESHMENTS:

The European Inn, on the route.
There are also other possibilities in Piddletrenthide and Piddlehinton.

Walk 42   **MARSHWOOD AND BETTISCOMBE**   5m (8km)

Maps: OS Sheets Landranger 193; Pathfinder 1316 and 1297.

A walk near one of Dorset's most famous hauntings.

Start: At 383996, Marshwood Church.

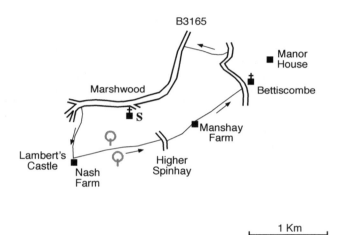

From the church walk back up to the main road (the B3165) and turn left along it, with great care, to reach the Bottle Inn. The inn is to the right: to the left and just a few yards further on there is a gate by a post box. Go through this gate and cross the field beyond to another gate. Go through and cross three further fields, using gates between them, to reach a gate on to a track opposite Nash Farm. To the right here is **Lambert's Castle**. Turn left, going immediately through a gate and following the track eastwards. Go through trees and over a stream to reach a gate. Go through and cross the field beyond to its far corner. Go through a gate there, cross a stream, go through a hedge gap and cross a field towards a farm to reach a lane. Cross and go up the farm drive for Higher Spinhay.

    Go to the left of the farm and cross a field to reach a track. Go left, through Manshay Farm, to reach a gate. Go through and cross the field beyond aiming for a large, distinctive oak tree. Continue down the field, crossing a stream at the bottom, then climbing across a field to reach a gate on to the road in **Bettiscombe**. Turn left along the village road, heading north towards the B3164. Where the road drops down a track goes off to the right: opposite this there is a gate: go through this and bear half-left across the field beyond to reach a gate. Go through, cross a stream and aim for a gap in the hedge ahead. Beyond this you cross a field to a gate and cross the field beyond to a gate on to the B3165. Turn left and, with care, walk back to **Marshwood**, turning left to return to the church.

POINTS OF INTEREST:

Lambert's Castle – The 'castle' of the name is the remains of an Iron Age hill fort.

Bettiscombe – This pretty hamlet lies below Pilsdon Pen, Dorset's highest point. Bettiscombe Manor, beyond the church, was built by the Pinney family whose wealth was based on West Indian plantations. Within the house is a skull which, legend has it, shrieks every time an attempt is made to remove it. Once when it was thrown into a pond the house itself was filled with shrieking until a diver retrieved it. Legend has it that it belonged to a West Indian slave, though one version of the tale says it belonged to the murdered servant of a Roman Catholic priest.

Marshwood – The view of Marshwood Vale from the village church is one of the best in Dorset. Indeed, Wordsworth claimed that this view (which he saw from the top of Pilsdon Pen) was the best in England.

REFRESHMENTS:

The Bottle Inn, Marshwood.

Walk 43   CONEY'S CASTLE   5m (8km)

Maps: OS Sheets Landranger 193; Pathfinder 1316.

Two old castles and some fine views.

Start: At 354986, a lay-by on the southern side of the B3165, near Wootten Cross.

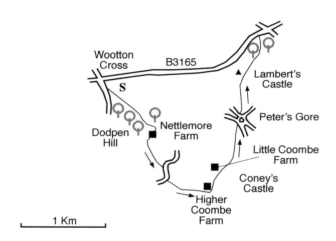

From the lay-by walk along the Wootton Cross and turn left along the road towards Wootton Fitzpaine. After a few yards there is a gate on the left: go through this and head diagonally across the field beyond to reach the edge of the woods on Dodpen Hill. Follow the wood edge – you may find it easier to walk just inside the woods – when the wood edge turns sharply right, go across the field ahead, bearing right to walk with a clump of woodland on your left hand to reach a gate on to a track. Turn right along the track to Nettlemore Farm. Go left through a gate and follow a path across two fields to reach a stile in the far right corner of the second. Go over on to a road.

Turn right along the road for 200 yards to reach a gate on the left. Go through and follow a path downhill to reach a footbridge over a stream that is a tributary of the River Char. Cross the bridge and follow the path up the far side of Great Combe to reach Higher Coombe Farm. Follow a track to the left of the farm buildings, to reach a more substantial track. Turn left along this, following it past Little Coombe Farm with the hill fort of **Coney's Castle** to the right.

The track reaches a curious meeting point of five roads known as Peter's Gore. Cross this junction to reach a signed path. Go through and follow the track for **Lambert's Castle**. The track reaches the old main entrance to the hill fort, from here a path crosses the fort and exits at the northern end. Follow the path as it descends through woodland to reach the B3165. Turn left and follow the road – its northern verge marks the boundary between Dorset and Somerset – with care back to the lay-by starting point.

POINTS OF INTEREST:

Coney's Castle/Lambert's Castle – Each of these hills is topped by a hill fort. Although many of these defensive positions have Neolithic or Bronze Age origins they are usually associated with the Iron Age, many of them having been constructed, or enlarged, by Celtic tribesmen. The basic hill fort consisted of a natural hill top further defended by a ditch and rampart, the latter topped by a wooden fence. As the slingshot replaced the spear more ditches and ramparts were added to keep attackers further away.

From each of the castles the views are outstanding, taking in the marvellous Marshwood Vale and the coast around Charmouth.

REFRESHMENTS:

None on the route, but available in nearby Marshwood and Hawkchurch.

Walk 44　　**MELBURY SAMPFORD**　　5m (8km)

Maps: OS Sheets Landranger 14; Pathfinder 1298.

A splendid parkland walk and a delightful village.

Start: At 573045, Evershot Church.

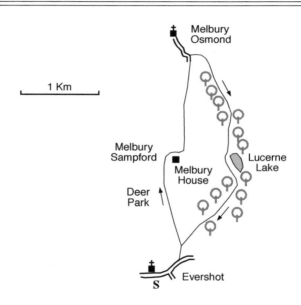

From the church walk along the village street towards Holywell, ignoring a turning to the right (to Maiden Newton) to reach the drive, to the left, for Melbury Park. Go between the lion-topped gate posts. After a few yards go ahead at a fork to walk through the park. Go through a kissing gate and walk to the rear of **Melbury House**, bearing right walk alongside it. Now go with the entrance drive as it turns left and heads northwards, following it through three gates to the end of a road. Ahead is **Melbury Osmond**, but that is a small diversion, our route going right at the road's sharp left turn. Follow the path under a bridge, bearing half-right to cross a stream. The stream has no bridge or ford and can be difficult to cross after heavy rain.

　　Go through a gate and cross the field beyond to another gate. Follow the track beyond the gate, with woodland to the right to reach a lane. Cross this, continuing along the track which now goes through a delightful piece of woodland. Go through a gate and continue, to reach a signed gate on the right. Go through and turn left along the field edge to reach a gate. Go through this and cross a stream to rejoin the track. Follow the track to a T-junction. Here, turn right on a signed path that soon reaches a track. Turn left along the track, with Lucerne Lake on your left, following it through another section of delightful woodland to reach a track junction. Turn right, following the track to reach the fork passed on the outward journey. Now turn left to follow the outward route back to **Evershot.**

POINTS OF INTEREST:

Melbury House – This huge house was built in the 16th century by the Strangways family, but has been modified and enlarged several times since. The hexagonal tower is original. Its purpose is not known, but most experts think that the large windows imply it was an observation tower for the deer park, believing that senior members of the Strangways family watched the hunting from it. The nearby chapel is older than the present house, dating from the 15th century. It has a collection of interesting memorials to the Strangways family including two alabaster effigies of knights in full armour.

Melbury Osmond – With its array of thatched cottages this is one of the prettiest villages in Dorset. In the church (dedicated to St Osmond, as might be expected) Thomas Hardy's mother and father were married in 1839. Sadly 50 years after the wedding the restorers were let loose. The couple would hardly recognise the place now.

Evershot – Evershot is beautifully positioned on a hill site that makes it one of Dorset's highest villages. The village inn, the *Acorn*, is the *Sow and Acorn* of Thomas Hardy's *Tess of the d'Urbervilles*. The link between the book and Tess' Cottage, opposite the church, is more tenuous.

REFRESHMENTS:
The Acorn Inn, Evershot.

Walk 45   **BADBURY RINGS** $5^1/_2$m (9km)

Maps: OS Sheets Landranger 195; Pathfinder 1300.

Easy farm track walking with a spectacular finale at Badbury Rings.

Start: At 962032, the National Trust car park at Badbury Rings.

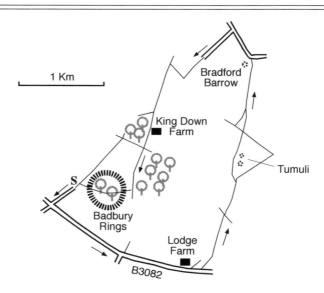

N.B. Dogs are not permitted within Badbury Rings itself at any time. An alternative final section of the walk is provided for those walking with dogs.

To set off, return to the main road and turn left. The grass border here is wide and the path well away from the traffic. Walk for a mile beside the impressive **Avenue of Beeches** before turning left at a farm track just after the one to Lodge Farm. At a junction after $^1/_2$ mile, go straight ahead, to the left of a barn, and up to a waymarked field gate. Go through it and head to the left of the tumulus on the skyline. (If the going looks heavy over the field, you may wish to stay on the track and make a left zig at the first junction and a right zag at the next.)

From the tumulus, continue to the small gate on the far side of the field. Cross the track beyond into the next field and go up to the gate in the left-hand corner. Rejoin the track and fork left at Bradford Barrow to walk along a narrow metalled lane. Shortly, turn left at a sign for Bradford Farm (not where it is shown on the Landranger map) and continue past the farm to reach a T-junction at Lambing Cottage. Turn right here, then left as you reach the line of the Roman road from Salisbury to Dorchester. The track rises towards a wood: keep to the left and pass King Down Farm, continuing until the track swings sharply to the left.

Those with dogs should turn right here, going into the wood and then turning left at a crossing on to a path that will take them directly to the car park.

Others take a path straight between two field gates. At the top of the slope the path is met by trees coming in from each side. At the end of the belt of trees there is a stile on the right with a 'No Dogs' sign: cross this and roam at will over the maze of footpaths on **Badbury Rings**. To return to the start just walk across the site as the car park is on the far (west) side.

POINTS OF INTEREST:

The Avenue of Beeches – The avenue was planted in 1835 and stretches from Kingston Lacy park gates to the (then) western edge of the estate. It was said that there were 365 trees on each side (one for each day of the year) – plus one (but on which side?) for Leap Years. Today's numbering of the trees starts at 001 on the south side going west and finishes at 649 at the east end of the north side.

Badbury Rings – The site is one of the largest Iron Age forts in the country. It has three concentric ditches and ramparts and is nearly a mile in circumference. Nearby there are Bronze Age barrows and part of the Roman road, Ackling Dyke (*see* Note to Walk 100). Many believe that Badbury is Mount Badon where King Arthur defeated the Saxons. At the entrance from the car park, there is a useful information table.

REFRESHMENTS:

There is nothing available on the walk, but in Wimborne, three miles to the east, there are several possibilities.

Walk 46   CHALBURY HILL AND HORTON   5¹/₂m (9km)

Maps: OS Sheets Landranger 195; Pathfinder 1301.
Farmland, woodland and a famous landmark.
Start: At 018069, a gravel lay-by on Chalbury Hill.

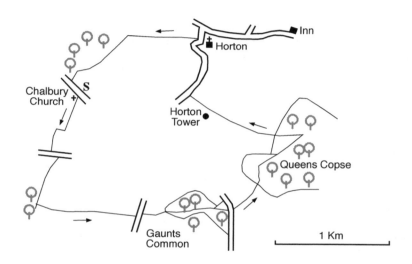

Make your way to **Chalbury Church** on top of the hill nearby. Now go through the gate and stile opposite the church porch and cross the field beyond half-right to reach another stile. The view from here is of the Allen valley, Hinton Martell church and the prominent Badbury Rings on the horizon. Go over the stile and follow a path over stiles and, after a right bend, cross another field diagonally towards the church tower. Drop down to a road and turn left along it for about 100 yards. Now turn right up a steepish bank through the trees. Cross a field and go over several stiles always keeping to the right-hand side of the fields. Hinton Martell village is down to the right. At a crossing path, where woodland starts, turn left and go over another stile beside a Wiltshire gate. Keep to the left of the fields, vaulting more stiles, to reach a farm and a road at Gaunt's Common. Opposite and just to the left, take the track for Holt Wood. After 100 yards, fork left, then go right into the Nature Reserve. The path

84

meanders eastward through pleasant woodland: cross a stream and, just after, keep to the right. Where the wood clears, follow a line of overhead wires, front right. The land can be a bit boggy as the route rises to reach a road. Take the broad gravel drive opposite and turn left after a few yards. Now go straight on to enter Queen's Copse. Keep left on a wide forest trail, descend slightly and go left at a junction. Carry on for $1/2$ mile or so and where the trail bends to the right, take a clear track back to the left, heading due west. After 300 yards, leave the woods and head across the fields to **Horton Tower**.

Beyond the tower, continue down to the road and turn right. The road drops, wiggles past a farm and continues to **Horton Church,** on the right. For refreshment, go another 100 yards, turn right and follow the road to Drusilla's, an inn, about $1/2$ mile away.

For the final stage of the walk, cross a small stile between two houses opposite the church gates. Go past a barn, join a farm track and go over the stile straight ahead. Walk up the right side of the field beyond to the point where a knuckle of trees/hedgerow juts out. Here, follow the waymarker left and across the field to reach a stile near the corner of the woods on the far side, heading south-west. Paths here are sometimes not reinstated after ploughing. Go through a steel gate and up through the fringe of woods to reach another gate. In the next field, keep left at first, then cross slightly uphill to a gateway where junior rugby posts stand incongruously. Now follow the track as it rises to the starting point.

POINTS OF INTEREST:
All Saints' Church, Chalbury – The church dates from 1291 but apparently had no dedication until 1946. It has a gallery and box pews and is beautifully situated on the hilltop.
Horton Tower – This famous folly landmark was built around 1750 for Humphrey Sturt, a local landowner, who is said to have followed deer-hunting from the 120 foot vantage point. It now houses a transmitter for a mobile telephone company. Access is not permitted.
St Wolfrida's Church, Horton – Founded in 1401, the church was almost entirely rebuilt in 1720-22. It is an unusual L-shape and has box-pews. The stone effigies within of Sir Giles de Braose and his first wife, Beatrice, date from the late 13th century.

REFRESHMENTS:
Drusilla's , Horton.

85

Walk 47   **Longham and the River Stour**   5¹/₂m (9km)

Maps: OS Sheets Landranger 195; Pathfinder 1334.

Level walking through river meadows and woods.

Start: At 068990, a lay-by on east side of A348 between Ferndown and Longham. Park clear of the recycling units.

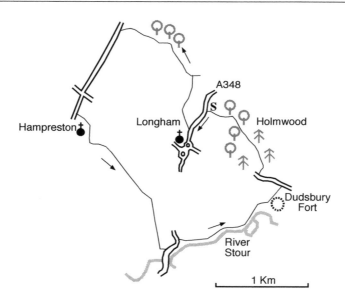

Go down to the left for 300 yards to reach a lane on the right. Before turning here, though, walk on for another 200 yards to see **Longham Church**, best viewed from the far side of the busy roundabouts. For future use, perhaps, the White Hart Inn is just down the road. Return to, and go up, Pompeys Lane. At some woods, fork right on to a bridleway and then go right again on to a better track. Go past Greenacres and continue to a T-junction. Turn left. Walk briefly beneath some power lines. The track bends left and then passes pleasant mixed woodland on the right. Knoll Gardens appear on the right - but that's another day out, so turn left at a road and follow it for ¹/₂ mile to reach the B3073.

Cross over towards Hampreston, going past the school, on the right, and forking left on to the church drive (Longham Bridge is $1^1/_4$m from here, not $2^1/_4$m as per signpost). Go left of the church and turn right past the back of the churchyard. Climb a stile, turn left and cross the river meadows, going under two sets of power lines. When a lane is reached, turn left and then go right into a field. Longham church spirelet is visible on the left. The path crosses three fields and then passes behind a large bungalow. Beyond this, climb another stile and look for a gate and stile on the right of the 'spur' of the next field, straight ahead. The grassy lane beyond leads out to the main road by Longham Bridge. Turn left, with care. Beyond the hotel and the Triangle building there is a path on the right to Dudsbury. The Kings Arms is 100 yards away at this point.

Take the footpath which soon brings you to a lovely $^1/_2$ mile or so stretch beside the **River Stour**. In summer you will be able to watch sand martins feeding over the weirs. Go over a footbridge and up the short hill in front. A stile and a path lead to a tarmac track across which is **Dudsbury Fort.** Turn left here and left again at a road. After 250 yards, take a sign-posted footpath on the right. Walk into Holmwood, go half-left and follow a path - indistinct at first beneath the pine needles, but marked by white splodges on the trees. In the wood, there are two main track junctions - fork left at each. Now, at a green patch, fork left back into the wood and follow yellow waymarkers, soon reaching a lane which leads out to the main road and the lay-by.

POINTS OF INTEREST:
Longham Church – This United Reform Church was built in 1841. The simple beauty of its architecture transcends even the noise and ugliness of its modern environment.
River Stour – The name rhymes with David Gower (!). The Stour is the longest river in Dorset. It rises in the National Trust gardens of Stourhead in Wiltshire and flows past Gillingham, Blandford and Wimborne before joining the Avon to enter the sea at Christchurch Harbour. The river is beloved by anglers and ornithologists.
Dudsbury Fort – This is an Iron Age hill fort with a single ditch and rampart.

REFRESHMENTS:
The Kings Arms, Longham.
The White Hart, Longham.

Walk 48 ALDERHOLT AND CRANBORNE COMMON 5^1/$_2$m (9km)
Maps: OS Sheets Landranger 195; Pathfinder 1282.

Through fields, lanes and common land near the Hampshire border.

Start: At 114125, the Churchill Arms, Alderholt.

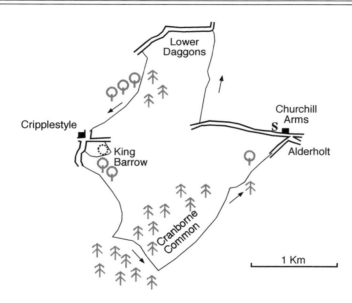

Parking in the Inn is for customers only, but parking is also available in nearby roads. Please park considerately.

Leave Alderholt by the Cranborne road and, after ^{1}/$_2$ mile, turn right, just past the church, on a path signposted to Bull Hill. Go over a stile and keep to the right side of two fields. Bend left at the top and exit over a stile on to a farm lane. Follow the lane to a road and turn left. Cross a brook and move westward into Hampshire, surprisingly. Turn left through Lower Daggons for 400 yards, then turn left up a farm track to walk back into Dorset. Fork right at the farm, following a bridleway. At the only bifurcation, keep right. A slight rise brings you out of the woods to reach a road by a house. Cross the road and continue on the bridleway, going through more woods down to reach a road at Cripplestyle.

At the junction on the main road, turn left, and after 100 yards, filter off to the right by a steel gate. Make your prickly way to the top of **King Barrow** which is visible from the road. Enjoy the view from its green tablecloth and then take a narrow path to the west - you arrived from the north. Cross a bridleway and walk past the right-hand edge of a belt of pines. Follow the path to a road and turn left. At the end of the metalled road is the site of the **Ebenezer chapel**. Continue along the track, keeping to the right of the ensuing field. Cross a bridge over the old Salisbury to Wimborne railway line (built in the 1860s) and go half-right and up in the next field to reach a gate in front of pine woods. A well-wheeled and well-hooved track leads left to Cranborne Common, a Dorset Nature Conservancy Trust area. Where a main track crosses, turn left and walk with small power lines overhead. The path is indistinct at times, but the lines and the odd yellow-topped post will bring you to a broad gravel track after about $1/2$ mile. Follow this track to the right. At some buildings, turn right and pass under larger power lines. Now follow the lane through pines and grass to reach a residential road and the starting point.

POINTS OF INTEREST:
King Barrow – Despite its name, archaeologists assure us that this is not a burial mound but a natural elevation.
Ebenezer Chapel – With touching simplicity, a plaque records the history of the chapel from its construction in 1807 to its collapse in 1976.

REFRESHMENTS:
The Churchill Arms, Alderholt.

Walk 49   ST ALDHELM'S HEAD $5^1/_2$m (9km)

Maps: OS Sheets Landranger 195; Outdoor Leisure 15.

A splendid coastal walk with fine views.

Start: At 974776, Worth Matravers car park.

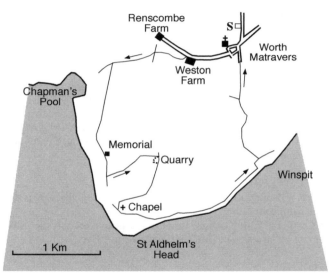

Turn right out of the car park and go down the road. Keep to the right to go through the village of **Worth Matravers**, passing the green and pond, on the left, and St Nicholas' Church, on the right. About 400 yards beyond the village a farm is reached: walk past it and immediately turn left, as signposted for 'St Aldhelm's Head'. After 30 yards turn right over a stile signposted 'Chapman's Pool'. Follow the path, crossing a track and a stile, and then taking a path with a stone waymarker for 'Chapman's Pool'. At the third stile turn immediately left to follow a path stone waymarked for 'St Aldhelm's Head'. Now walk along the escarpment, with a fine panoramic view of Chapman's Pool, below, and the coastline to Weymouth and Portland Bill.

    After $^3/_4$ mile, beyond a small memorial garden with a stone table and bench to commemorate the Royal Marines killed in action between 1945 and 1990, descend some 50 steps into Pier Bottom, and take the path up the combe on the left. (The energetic may prefer to keep straight on, going up the 100 plus steps and following a short cliff walk to the coastguard station.) At the top of the combe there is a small quarry on the right: go over the stile here and turn immediately left. After about 50 yards, at the junction with a bridlepath, turn right on a path signposted 'St Aldhelm Head $^3/_4$'. Walk to the chapel and disused coastguard station at **St Aldhelm's Head**. Turn left and follow the path, with great care, along the cliff edge to reach the old quarry workings at **Winspit**. From here there is a fine view along the coast to Anvil Point Lighthouse.

In the bottom the cliff path meets a track: turn left and follow the valley inland. After $^1/_2$ mile, at the water treatment plant, take the right fork and follow the path up and across a large field to reach the village. Now keep the green and the pond on the left to return to the car park.

POINTS OF INTEREST:
Worth Matravers – This is an attractive village, with stone built houses centred around the village pond and green. The Church of St Nicholas dates from about 1100. Benjamin Jesty the first known person to inoculate his family against smallpox by infecting them with cowpox (1774) is buried here. Despite the acclaim given to Jenner at Berkeley in Gloucestershire, the claim in Jesty's epitaph is true.
St Aldhelm's Head – The headland, sometimes known as St Alban's Head, is named for St Aldhelm, the first bishop of Sherborne. The chapel, dedicated to the saint, dates from Norman times. Many have wondered whether, with its thick walls and remote location, it really was a chapel, but there is a legend that it was built by a Norman knight who stood here to wave farewell to his son (or daughter) who was sailing to Normandy on honeymoon and could only watch, horror-struck as the newly-weds were drowned when their ship floundered on the rocks below. The knight built the chapel as a memorial and to carry a light to warn ships. From the top of the old coastguard station, 350 feet above sea level, it is claimed that the water tower above Cherbourg can be seen on an exceptionally clear day.
Winspit – The remains are of extensive quarrying which ceased about 50 years ago.

REFRESHMENTS:
The Square and Compass Inn, Worth Matravers.
There is also a café and a tearoom in Worth Matravers.

Walk 50   KIMMERIDGE CLIFF AND SWYRE HEAD   5^1/$_2$m (9km)

Maps: OS Sheets Landranger 195; Outdoor Leisure 15.

A coastal walk with a stiff climb, but outstanding views.

Start: At 918801, the Quarry car park above Kimmeridge.

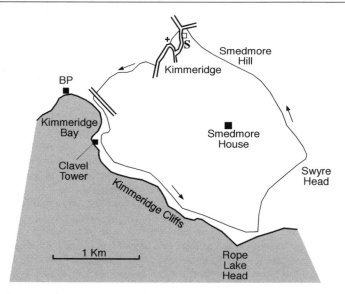

Leave the car park and turn right to the road junction. Go over the stile on the left signposted 'Kimmeridge ^{1}/$_4$' and go down the steep field beyond. Go through the churchyard and walk down **Kimmeridge** village street. Go over the stile signposted 'To the Sea' immediately after the last cottage on the right. The path beyond goes down the right-hand side of a field to reach a double stile at the bottom turn left. Go over and keep to the edges of two fields to reach a road. Turn left, walk past a toilet block and, after 50 yards, turn right on to the cliff path above Kimmeridge Bay. To the right from here is BP's Kimmeridge Well site.

Turn right at the far end, by another toilet block, on to a road signposted 'Coast Path'. After a further 75 yards, turn left up the steps signposted 'Coastal Path', reaching the **Clavel Tower** at the top. The route now follows the Coastal Path for 1^1/$_2$ miles, staying with the cliff edge until a stone waymarker for 'Swyre Head ^{3}/$_4$' is reached by

Rope Lake Head. Here, go over the stile and up the field edge. The path gets progressively steeper and the last 200 yards to the summit of Swyre Head (at 666 feet – 203 metres – the highest point on the Isle of Purbeck) are extremely steep. To compensate, the walker is rewarded with a magnificent view of the coast from St Aldhelm's Head to Portland and, inland, of Corfe Castle, Poole Harbour and beyond.

From the top, turn left past the trig. point and follow a path beside the wall at the edge of the escarpment to Smedmore Hill. Continue along the same path which leads directly to the cross-roads near the starting car park.

POINTS OF INTEREST:

Kimmeridge – This attractive village of stone and thatch is part of the Smedmore Estate which has been in the Clavel (and then Mansel by marriage) family for over 500 years.

The shale of the cliffs, formerly known as Kimmeridge coal has been burnt by locals in the past as cheap fuel. In the 19th century, several attempts were made to mine and extract the oil and gas from the shale but none were commercially successful.

Clavel Tower – The tower is a now-dangerous ruin built in 1820 by the Rev Richards of Kimmeridge and named for the Clavel family from whom the vicar had descended. Richards changed his name to Clavel when he inherited the Smedmore Estate. The tower's purpose is unknown: probably it was just a folly.

REFRESHMENTS:

None on the route, but the Kimmeridge Post Office offers a limited range.

Maps: OS Sheets Landranger 193 and 194; Pathfinder 1298.
A quiet walk near the Somerset border.
Start: At 489056, the church, Cheddington.

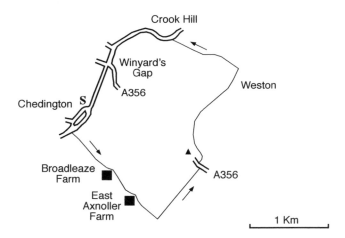

From the church walk south-westwards (away from the A356 and the village inn) along the road towards Mosterton. Walk through the village to reach a road junction. Turn right, but almost immediately turn left to cross the road into the drive for Broadleaze Farm. Follow the drive, which crosses two bridges over streams that will join a little way to the west to create the River Axe. At the farm, walk to the left of the buildings to reach a gate into a field. Cross the field to a gate. Go through and half-left to reach a gap through some trees. Now descend to cross a stream, and climb up towards East Axnoller Farm to reach a gate. Go through and turn left through the farmyard to reach a gate.

Follow the track beyond as it bears right to another gate. Go through this, cross a track and go through another gate. Walk to yet another gate, beyond which bear left to reach a track. Bear left along the track to a gate into a field. Go half-left to a hedge gap and cross the field beyond to another hedge gap. Go through this gap to reach the main A356. Cross, with great care, turn left and then right through the first gate towards a farm. Bear left of the farm to a gate: to the left here is a somewhat sad trig. point. Go through the gate and descend into a valley to reach another gate. Follow the track beyond to reach a gate into a farm. Go through and follow a lane through the hamlet of Weston.

Where the lane bears right, go left to reach a gate. Go through and bear half-left, following a hedge downhill. Go over a stream, then climb up a field, with a hedge on your right, to reach a gate. Go through and continue climbing, heading towards Crook Hill to reach a gate on to a road. Go through and turn left. Bear left at a junction and walk down to the road's junction with the A356 at **Winyard's Gap**. Cross, with care, and take the road past the Winyard's Gap Inn to return to **Cheddington**, bearing right in the village to reach the church.

POINTS OF INTEREST:

Winyard's Gap – This cutting through the chalk hills on the Dorset-Somerset border has been well-known for centuries. Most famously it was used by King Charles I in 1644. Today it takes the A356 from Crewkerne to Dorchester.

The monument at the Gap is to the 43rd Division of the Wessex Regiment which, 300 years after Charles' army had passed through, distinguished itself in the service of another King at the battle for Normandy in 1944.

Cheddington – This beautiful village, with its church and fine collection of thatched cottages, set on chalk hills overlooking pastoral peace, is the epitome of Englishness.

REFRESHMENTS:
The Winyard's Gap Inn, on the route.

Walk 52　　　**TOLLER PORCORUM**　　　$5^1/_2$m (9km)

Maps: OS Sheets Landranger 194; Pathfinder 1317.
A fine walk in the Hooke valley.
Start: At 561980, Toller Porcorum Church.

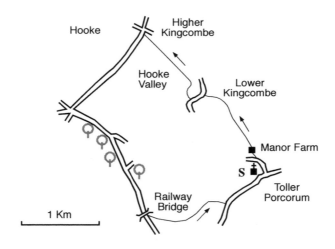

Go eastwards along the village street (that is, stand with the church behind you and turn left). At the road junction turn left towards Hooke. At the end of the houses on the right, turn right on a bridleway for Lower Kingcombe. After a few yards turn left through a gate into Manor Farm. Go through the farm to a gate on to a track. Follow the track through a field to a gate. Cross the field beyond to a gate on to another track. Follow the track to reach a road at Lower Kingcombe, ignoring stiles, and a track to the right, along the way.

Turn left, crossing the River Hooke to reach a waymarked gate on the right. Follow the waymarked posts in the field beyond, bearing right to reach a footbridge over the River Hooke. Cross the bridge and turn left to reach a stile. Go over and bear right across a field to reach another stile. Cross the field beyond to a gate, and the field beyond that to a stile. Go over and walk past a pond to reach a gate on to a lane at Higher Kingcombe. Go down the lane to a road and turn left. Follow the road – which leads to Powerstock – to reach a cross-roads. Turn left on a road signed for Toller Porcorum.

At the next junction turn right to walk downhill to an old railway bridge. Go under the bridge and go through the signed gate on the left just beyond. Go half-right across the field beyond to reach a gate. Go through and turn left to cross a tributary stream of the Hooke. Go through a gate and cross a field to a stile. Go over and bear right to reach a gate on to a road. Turn left into **Toller Porcorum**, walking through the village to regain the church.

POINTS OF INTEREST:

Toller Porcorum – It seems a shame that this beautifully-sited village, with one of the most romantic names in Dorset, should derive the second part of its name from the pigs that once thrived in the wooded Hooke valley. The first part of the name derives from Knights Hospitallers, the Brethren of the Order of St John of Jerusalem who owned the village, and nearby Toller Fratrum. The village church, set on a little hill, has a fine 15th-century tower.

REFRESHMENTS:
The Old Swan Inn, Toller Porcorum.

Maps: OS Sheets Landranger 194; Pathfinder 1299.
A visit to a crossing point of ancient tracks.
Start: At 728032, Folly Farm.

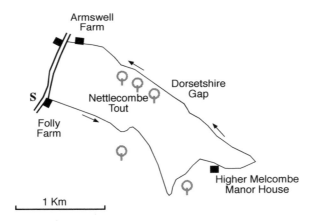

The start is on the minor road that links Plush and Mappowder, two tiny villages that lie east of the Piddle Valley. To reach Plush, take the Alton Pancras road (the B3143) through Piddletrenthide and turn right. In Plush, turn right again for Mappowder. Parking is not easy, but with care can be organised on the verges between Folly Farm and Armswell Farm, which is also on the route.

Go eastwards, uphill, along the track from Folly Farm. Where the track forks, bear left passing a clump of trees and continuing to a gate. Go through and follow the hedge to the left. Where it ends, turn left and cross a field to a water tank. Turn right and follow the field edge to reach a gate in the corner. Go through and follow the track beyond, going through two gates and continuing past trees, on the left. Just beyond the last tree there is a gate on the left. Go through this and another shortly after. Follow the path as it descends, ignoring a gate on the left to continue to one straight ahead. Go through and walk with a hedge on your right hand. Do not go through the gate in this hedge: instead, continue down the hill to reach a facing gate. Now turn right over a stile and follow the hedge to your left to reach a gate, also on the left, on to a track. Follow the track to a lane and turn right, soon passing **Higher Melcombe Manor House**. About 300 yards beyond the House you will reach three gates on the left. The centre one is signed for Dorset Gap: go through and turn left along a hedge to reach a gate in the field's far corner. Go through, cross a track to a gate and follow the left hedge in the field beyond. Go through a gate on to a track and follow this through another gate to where it forks. Bear right to reach a cross-ways of tracks at **Dorsetshire Gap**.

Take the track signed for Armswell Farm (the second from the left) going through trees to a gate. Follow the path beyond, forking left where it divides to climb up past trees. Bear right, but soon turn left through a gate, crossing the track beyond to reach another gate. Follow the path beyond, bearing left when another joins from the right and going through a gate to reach buildings of Armswell Farm. Go to the left of the buildings to reach a gate on the right. Go through and turn left along the farm drive to reach a road opposite the farm itself. Turn left to return to the start.

POINTS OF INTEREST:

Higher Melcombe Manor House – The house has a long history as there is evidence of a Norman hill on the site. The present house dates, in part, from the late 16th century, but has been much modified.

Dorsetshire Gap – This nick in the hills that form the southern edge of the Blackmoor Vale has been a crossing point since men first had a need to travel. All the routes that course here are ancient trackways, giving a fine sense of the continuity of landscape history.

REFRESHMENTS:

None on the route, but available in Piddletrenthide, to the south, and Hazelbury Bryan, to the north.

Walk 54   PUDDLETOWN FOREST $5^1/2$m (9km)

Maps: OS Sheets Landranger 194; Pathfinder 1318.

The heart of 'Hardy Country'.

Start: At 724923, the car park at Higher Bockhampton.

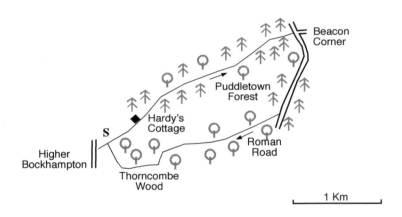

Every walk in Dorset could claim to be in Hardy Country, but this one, which visits Thomas Hardy's birth place, has the best claim of all. The start point is reached from the A35 just a couple of miles north-east of Dorchester.

From the car park, take the path signed for **Hardy's Cottage**. Turn left at the next signpost, then bear right with the path to reach the Cottage. Turn right and follow the blue waymarker past the vehicle barrier into Puddletown Forest. Follow further blue waymarkers in the forest, ignoring side turnings to maintain a north-easterly direction. The path descends gently into Tolpuddle Hollow, then rises to reach another vehicle barrier at a road at Beacon Corner.

Turn right along the road side for $^3/4$ mile, descending gently, to reach a point where an old Roman road crosses the new road. The crossing is not marked, but is very obvious. Turn right here, following the broad track – a forestry road now follows the course of the Roman road – through the trees. Again, ignore all side turnings to reach an area of open heath. The old road is less distinct, but still quite obvious, as it crosses this area of heather to reach a junction of six tracks close to a pond. Taking the second turn right here follows a path known as Snail's Creep back to Hardy's Cottage. The name apparently recalls the use of the path by smugglers who made their way slowly and quietly through the forest.

The better route is to turn left on a path heading a litte west of south. After about 200 yards you will reach another path junction. Here, turn right on a path that follows the edge of Black Heath to reach Thorncombe Wood. Bear right at a fork in the path and follow it down to reach a track. Turn left on this to return to the start point.

POINTS OF INTEREST:

Hardy's Cottage – The small two-storey thatched cottage was built by Thomas Hardy's grandfather in 1800. Here, on 2 June 1840, Thomas was born. Here, too, he wrote *Under the Greenwood Tree* and *Far from the Madding Crowd*, two of his best known books. Both Hardy's father and grandfather were members of the church choir at nearby Stinsford, Hardy's original title for *Under the Greenwood Tree* having been *The Mellstock Quire*, using the original spelling for choir.

Black Heath/Thorncombe Wood – The 46 acres of wood and heath are owned by Dorset County Council and maintained as a nature reserve. The area is criss-crossed by paths and has a good supply of information boards. A leaflet is available from Tourist Offices.

REFRESHMENTS:

None on the route, so bring your own and make use of the picnic area, or take a short drive to Dorchester where there are numerous possibilities.

Walk 55   **BERE REGIS**   5^1/$_2$m (9km)

Maps: OS Sheets Landranger 194; Outdoor Leisure 15.
A fine heathland walk.
Start: At 847947, Bere Regis Churchyard.

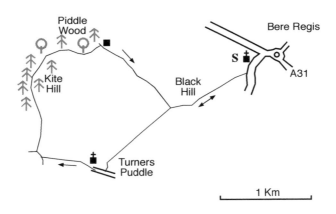

From the churchyard, walk along the right-hand side of the church to reach a gate on to a road. Turn right, cross a bridge over a tributary of the River Piddle and turn right again to go along Southbrook. Bear left with the road, but where it goes right, walk ahead along a path which passes a cemetery, to the left. Bear right, following blue waymarkers, near some oak trees, and follow a path uphill across the **heath** of Black Hill. Go straight over at two path junctions, continuing to reach a gate. Go through, bearing left beyond to pass a farm, and continuing to reach a crossing track. Turn right to reach a lane and follow it through the hamlet of **Turners Puddle**.

The route is now following the Piddle Valley: maintain direction, with the river to your left. A track joins from the left: continue for about 100 yards, then turn right through a gate and follow a track uphill along the right edge of a field. Go through a gate and continue to a fork. Take the left-hand branch (as waymarked in blue) into the

Kite Hill conifer plantation. Walk through the trees to reach a path junction. Turn right along a bridleway, going through a gate and continuing through, then along, the edge of Piddle Wood. Go through a gate to reach a T-junction of paths. Turn right, passing a farm to the left to reach another gate. Go through and follow the track beyond, going over at a cross-tracks to reach the heathland of Black Hill again. At a track fork, take the left-hand branch and continue to reach a track junction passed on the outward route. Now turn left to follow the outward route back to **Bere Regis** and the start.

POINTS OF INTEREST:

Heath – The finest heaths in England are to be found in Dorset. Heath forms on a base of sand or gravel that allows rapid percolation of water from the surface. This percolation removes nutrients, leaving a poor, acidic soil on which a surface layer of humus from recently decomposed plant life forms. The Dorset heathlands support the Dartford warbler, the smooth snake and a specific form of heather. Sadly, during this century some 85% of Dorset's heathland has been destroyed. The heath on this walk is one of the best remaining sections.

Turners Puddle – This almost deserted hamlet with its abandoned church typifies the migration of Dorset folk to the towns.

Bere Regis – The village has a long history, the Saxon Queen Elfrida being abbess of a nunnery here in the 10th century. The royal addition to the name derives from a later period of history, the Middle Ages, when King John had a house in the town and stopped on his way to and from the royal hunting grounds on Powerstock Common. Other kings followed his lead, though a disastrous fire later wiped out medieval Bere. The village church is well-known in architectural circles for its nave roof constructed in the late 15th century by Cardinal Morton, a local man who became Henry VIII's Lord Chancellor. The roof is of unique design, a complicated array of curved and straight beams from which the twelve Apostles (dressed as Tudor gentlemen) stare down. The church also houses several memorials to members of the Turbervilles, the family which inspired Thomas Hardy's *Tess of the d'Urbervilles*. In the book the village is called Kingsbere.

REFRESHMENTS:
There are numerous possibilities in Bere Regis.

TARRANT GUNVILLE 6m (9¹/₂km)
or 9m (14¹/₂km)

Maps: OS Sheets Landranger 195; Pathfinder 1281.
A farmland walk with fine views and a long barrow or two.
Start: At 926127, the Bugle Horn Inn.

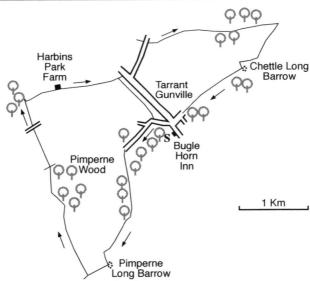

From the inn, go left for 150 yards, then turn left again (there is some very limited alternative parking space at the church entrance for those who are not patrons of the inn). Go up the hill passing **Gunville Manor** on the left. At a road junction, go straight on, following the Home Farm sign. After 600 yards, fork left down a stony track signposted to Westbury Lodge. The dark lane dips and rises and becomes grassy as it emerges into daylight. Go through a gate with woodland (Hinton Bushes) on the right, then keep straight on through another gate. At the end of the woods, turn half-right and make for the obvious shape of **Pimperne Long Barrow**. From the barrow, there is an excellent all-round view of the Dorset farmland. Blandford Camp is nearby to the south. On the west side of the barrow, find a gap in the hedge and follow the path beyond. At an old silage pit, turn right beyond the hedge and follow the track through broad fields for about 2 miles - you may see hare and roe deer here - passing Pimperne Wood with its variety of broad-leaved trees. Go through a large double field gate and cross a narrow road to reach a wide, green lane. After 400 yards, with woods on the left, turn right down to Harbins Park Farm. Where the farm road bends right, carry straight on, going gently downhill through fields.

Just after a small, discreet sewage station on the left, the shorter route turns right over a stile and follows the left edge of successive fields, going over three stiles. On reaching a road, turn left downhill to reach Tarrant Gunville and the Bugle Horn.

For the longer walk, continue down the track, passing chicken farm buildings to reach a road. Turn right and soon left to pass more poultry buildings. Walk up the road to reach a junction. Turn right on to a grassy path which rises through high-banked hedges to reach a crossing with a metalled farm road. Go straight over and follow the track past woods, firstly on the right and then on the left. After about $3/4$ mile, there is a large barn on the right: turn back behind this and keep to the left edge of a large field. From the field's high point there are fine views, with the tree-topped Pentridge Hill in the north-east. At the end of the field, turn right behind the hedge. Now bend left and, just before some overhead wires, turn right over a waymarked stile. Here on the left beneath the trees and undergrowth is Chettle Long Barrow (*see* Note to Walk 66). Continue down the side of the field and cross a metalled track to reach a grassy lane. The lane leads to a superb beech avenue from the lower end of which you can look left to see **Eastbury House**. Go through a kissing gate and a short belt of woodland to reach School Lane: drop down to the village road and turn left for the Bugle Horn.

POINTS OF INTEREST:

Gunville Manor – In the early 19th century, the house was occupied by Josiah Wedgwood of the Potteries. It is not open to the public.

Pimperne Long Barrow – A Neolithic earthen barrow 350 feet long and 9 feet high. It is enhanced by its commanding position and is regarded as one of the finest examples in the country.

Eastbury House – Designed by Vanburgh and completed in 1738 for George Bubb Dodington, the house was demolished on the owner's death 30 years later when his heirs were unable to find a buyer. Only the old servant quarters remain. The house is private.

REFRESHMENTS:

The Bugle Horn Inn, Tarrant Gunville. The bugle horn of the name is the crest of the Dodington family of Eastbury House.

Walk 58 Sixpenny Handley and Chase Woods 6m (9¹/₂km)
Maps: OS Sheets Landranger 184; Pathfinder 1281.
An introduction to the woods of Cranborne Chase.
Start: At 994173, Sixpenny Handley school.

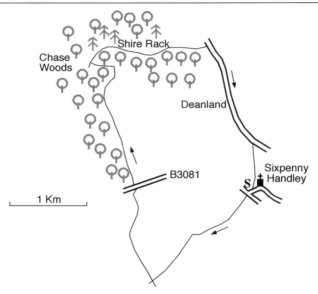

Parking is not easy in the village – please be considerate. At the top (west) end, there is some space between the school and the church.

Opposite the school, take the bridleway to Dean, going down to the left of Park Cottage. The way is stony at first, then chalky, as it leads into a field. Next, a dip on a left-hand bend brings you to a gate: go through and turn right along a grassy path which is followed to reach the B3081 by a small stable building. Cross the road and go over the two stiles opposite. Proceed up the side of the field beyond, hugging the wood and crossing a number of stiles. At any time in this middle section of the walk, the gregarious fallow deer may be seen, but this is especially likely in winter when the visibility is improved through the bare woodland. After a mile, at a barred stile, the right of way goes half-right across the middle of a large field to reach a stile hidden from view by a convex slope. In the absence of a directional waymarker or a clearly trodden path across the field, it may be better to continue round the edge of the field to reach the stile. Over the stile, turn left into Chase Woods, one of the few remaining wooded areas of the once thickly forested **Cranborne Chase**.

After 400 yards, turn right along Shire Rack, one of the Chase's ancient tracks. The track passes through conifers and coppiced birch then drops to cross another path. Beyond, it rises and then, rather unexpectedly, meets fields on the left. This mile of Shire Rack, as the name suggests, clings to the county boundary: you are now walking only inches from Wiltshire. Continuing through broad-leaved trees, the path eases down to a gravelly track. When the head of the road is reached, turn right and walk through straggling Deanland. After about a mile of roadway there is a large gap in the hedge on the right. The gap is waymarked in yellow – do not follow the blue waymarker passed just before the gap. The path angles beside a barbed-wire fence and into a field where the route is helpfully marked by posts. About 50 yards into the next field, turn right for Sixpenny Handley church. Inside and beside the churchyard gate, a barely legible gravestone inscription relates how, in lawless times of yore, poached deer were hidden within, pending their surreptitious disposal. Beyond the church, the lych gate opens on to the village street of Sixpenny Handley. Turn right to return to the school.

POINTS OF INTEREST:

Cranborne Chase – This hunting preserve dates from the time of William the Conqueror. It was bestowed on Robert Cecil, 1st Earl of Salisbury, by James I and remained in his family's keeping until 1828. The Chase's forests used to cover about 500 square miles of north-east Dorset and adjoining counties. In the 18th and 19th centuries, it was a region infamous for the lawlessness of poachers and robbers. Today, the thick woods around Ashmore, Tollard Royal and Sixpenny Handley - roughly the area of the ancient Inner Chase - are generally regarded as forming the Chase.

Sixpenny Handley – Like other Dorset place names of the same coin (Shillingstone, Poundbury, even Purse Caundle), the name of Sixpenny Handley is not of financial derivation. Two Saxon hundreds of Saxpena and Hanlega gave their names to the village and refer to its high position in a forest clearing. The village, known locally as Handley, was rebuilt after complete destruction by fire in 1892. There is a centenary memorial stone by the church gate.

REFRESHMENTS:
The Star Inn, Sixpenny Handley.
The Roebuck Inn, Sixpenny Handley.

Maps: OS Sheets Landranger 195; Pathfinder 1282.

A comfortable walk from a pretty village to ancient earthworks.
Start: At 031120, on the stony roadside verge opposite Wimborne
St Giles school. Do not park on the grass.

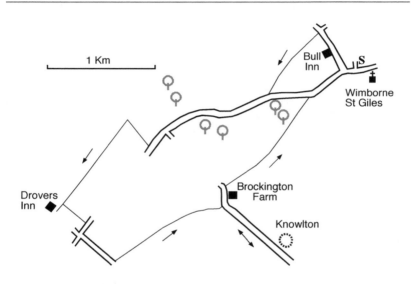

Across the green of **Wimborne St Giles** are the almshouses and the church. Start in
the opposite direction, going past the old stocks and turning right over the bridge. Note
the Bull Inn for later refreshment. Turn left on a track where a road comes in from the
right. Keep to the right of the field to reach a wooded strip. Turn right along a road,
following it for about ³/₄ mile. Horton Tower (*see* Note to Walk 46), visible for much
of this walk, is on the left. About 300 yards after a road junction, turn right on to a
farm track. Turn left past a vehicle barrier and go down a broad greenway for over ¹/₂
mile. As the way narrows, turn left on to a path (the Drovers Inn is just a few yards
ahead) which is confined at first, but then goes straight across a field. Turn right on the
road down to Amen Corner and turn left towards Bowerswain. As you approach the
farm, turn left by the Gussage stream. The path soon bears left away from the stream

and proceeds, mainly covered, for nearly a mile up to Brockington Farm. Turn right along the road over the Allen river and up to the earthworks at **Knowlton**.

Return to and wriggle past Brockington Farm, turning right up a farm track shortly beyond it. Go past a 'Private' sign on the right at a junction and continue ahead, going up the side of a field to reach a small wood at the end. Negotiate a Wiltshire gate and two stiles to the right. The wide and rough grassy track beyond leads to a road, just before which St Giles House can be seen in the trees to the right. Turn right along the road down to a junction. The inn is to the left here, while the start point is straight on.

POINTS OF INTEREST:

Wimborne St Giles – St Giles House (not open to the public) dates from 1650, the almshouses from 1624. Both were built by Anthony Ashley Cooper, 1st Earl of Shaftesbury. The 7th Earl, the Victorian social reformer, is commemorated by the statue of Eros in Piccadilly Circus in London. The village church was built in 1732 and contains the Ashley family pew and memorials. In the churchyard are the 17th-century gravestones of family servants.

Knowlton Earthworks and Church – The three Bronze Age circles here date from about 2,500 BC. Two of them are barely discernible. Inside the third, the ruined church of flint and stone has a Norman nave and a 14th-century tower. It is thought that the church ceased to be used from about 1600 when the local community dwindled and eventually expired.

REFRESHMENTS:
The Drovers Inn, Gussage All Saints.
The Bull Inn, Wimborne St Giles.

Walk 60   CHILCOMBE AND ASKERSWELL   6m (9¹/₂km)

Maps: OS Sheets Landranger 194; Pathfinder 1317.

An interesting walk on the Downs north of Chesil Beach.

Start: At 530926, Askerswell Church.

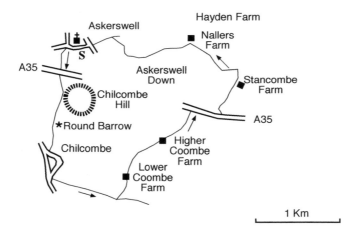

Walk westwards along the street (that is turn right if your back is to the church) to reach a junction with a village street going right. To the left here a signed path crosses fields, running southwards and downhill to reach the A35. Cross the embanked road with great care to reach a short track heading up towards Chilcombe Hill. From this the footpath heads south again, contouring below the ramparts of the Iron Age hill fort that tops the hill, then passing a round barrow built by earlier, Bronze Age, dwellers on the hill. Beyond the barrow the path drops down to meet a bridleway. Bear right along this to reach a lane. Turn left along this, going through **Chilcombe** to reach a road.

At the point where the lane reaches the road there is a gate (on the lane) to the left. Go through this and follow the bridleway beyond as it descends to a stream, a tributary of the River Bride. Cross the stream, go through a gate and the small belt of trees and climb up the far valley side. Soon, the bridleway reaches a crossing path.

Turn left here, following the path to a track. Turn left, following the track past Lower Coombe Farm and on to Higher Coombe Farm. From the farm the track rises steeply to reach the main A35. Turn right along the road, taking great care, and even more care when crossing the road to reach a signed track for Stancombe Farm.

Walk through the farm, but then leave the track by turning left along a path that contours around the edge of Haydon Down, maintaining height above the trees and stream in the valley to the left. The path heads for Nollers Farm, soon visible ahead. At the farm, turn left along the farm drive. This drops to cross the stream, then rises up Askerswell Down. Follow the track, passing a couple of houses, then descending slightly to reach a T-junction with a lane. Turn left along the lane to reach a road junction. Now walk ahead back to **Askerswell** and the church.

POINTS OF INTEREST:

Chilcombe – This beautifully situated village has a church that claims to be one of the smallest in England. The building was built originally in the 13th century, but has been modified several times. It has no tower or spire and a churchyard that is barely the size of a tennis court. Inside there is a painted panel which is claimed to have been washed ashore at West Bexington from one of the ships of the Spanish Armada that had floundered in the Channel.

Askerswell – This charming village retains an air of tranquillity despite the closeness of the busy A35. The church was rebuilt in the mid-19th century, only the medieval tower escaping the restorers.

REFRESHMENTS:

None on the route, but *The Spyway Inn* lies just a short way north of Askerswell.

Walk 61   **LYME REGIS AND CHARMOUTH**   6m (9½km)
Maps: OS Sheets Landranger 193; Pathfinder 1316.
A walk below one of the most important cliffs in Britain.
Start: At 343921, Buddle Bridge, Lyme Regis.

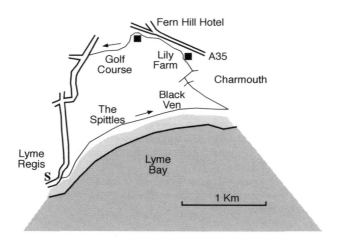

The very best way to link Lyme Regis and Charmouth is along the beach. However, this is also the most dangerous route as the cliffs are extremely unstable and unclimbable, and high tide fills the coves. It is imperative, therefore, that the beach is walked on a falling tide. Please check the local tide table. Do not guess the state of the tide – the sea does not take prisoners.

From the bridge make your way down to the beach and turn left along it. On the beach below the **cliffs** of the Spittles and Black Ven you will find numerous ammonites in the rocks that have fallen from above. The beach walk ends at the mouth of the River Char. Just this side of the Heritage Coast Centre a signed path behind the beach huts goes uphill to reach Old Lyme Road. Cross this and go up a lane to reach a junction. Turn right, but after 50 yards go left through a waymarked gate. Follow the path beyond through several fields to reach a gate. Go through on to a path that runs beside the main road. Turn left along the path to reach the Fern Hill Hotel.

Go past the hotel, then turn left on a signed path through trees to reach a golf course. Cross the course on a path signed by white stones set in the grass, to reach the main road again. Turn left, with care, but soon go left off the road in to Timber Hill. Where the road goes sharply right, turn left along a lane. After a few yards go through a signed kissing gate on the right and cross the field beyond to reach another. Go through and bear half-right across a field to reach a stile. Go over and cross a field to another stile. Go over on to the main road. Turn left and follow the road through **Lyme Regis** to return to Buddle Bridge.

POINTS OF INTEREST:
Cliffs – The cliffs of Lyme Bay are of blue lias, a sedimentary rock laid down below seas of the Jurassic era. For centuries ammonites, the coiled fossils of all sizes that can be seen in the rocks on the beach, had been found by locals, but in 1810 Mary Anning, an 11-year-old, found a new form of fossil. It took her ten years to unearth the fossil which proved to be the first ichthyosaur to have been uncovered. Mary sold it to the British Museum for £23. Later Mary Anning discovered the plesiosaur, another marine reptile. Today the cliffs still reveal fossils – though indiscriminate hammering is discouraged on the grounds of both safety and the damage that can result to potentially important discoveries. If you want a local fossil it is best to visit the Fossil shops in Lyme Regis.

Lyme Regis – Famous for its Cobb, which features in the film of John Fowles' *The French Lieutentant's Woman*, the town has many other interesting features. Monmouth House is where the Duke of Monmouth stayed before moving on to defeat at the Battle of Sedgemoor.

REFRESHMENTS:
There are many possibilities in Lyme Regis and Charmouth.

Walk 62   **POWERSTOCK COMMON**   6m (9^1/$_2$km)

Maps: OS Sheets Landranger 194; Pathfinder 1317.

A fine hill fort, with magnificent views.

Start: At 548948, the Shatcombe Lane car park/picnic area.

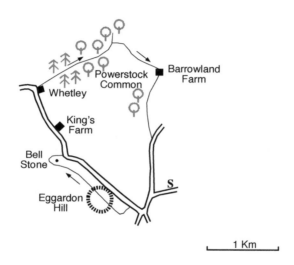

The start point lies just off the minor road that links Toller Porcorum and the A356 with Spyway, Askerswell and the A35.

From the car park walk back to the Spyway/Toller Porcorum road and turn left. Walk down the road to a junction and turn right there on the road for Powerstock. Go along the road for 200 yards to reach a waymarked gate on the left. Head south-westward, but leave the path at the entrance to the **Eggardon Hill** fort, going over the right-hand of two stiles on the right and walking across the fort. Go through the western ramparts and follow a path along the steep-sided hill spur. Now scramble down the spur's steep edge to reach the **Bell Stone**.

From the Bell Stone continue westwards for 100 yards to reach a track and turn right along this climbing over the final nose of the hill spur to reach another track. Turn right along this to reach a lane. Go left along the lane. Go past King's Farm

114

to reach the hamlet of Whetley. Go past Whetley Farm to reach a signed bridleway for Stones Common. Turn right (north-east) along this crossing two fields to reach wooded **Powerstock Common**. The woodland starts with a conifer plantation, but soon becomes more ancient, with fine clumps of oak, ash and hazel. After the bridleway emerges from the forest it goes gently uphill. At the top of this climb there is a waymarked gate on the right. Go through this and go downhill across a field to reach another gate in its bottom corner. Go through on to a track to Barrowland Farm. At the farm turn right along a track to the right of the farmhouse. Go through the gate at the track's end and cross the field beyond to reach a gate in its far corner. Go through and follow the right edge of the field beyond, maintaining direction when this curves right to reach a gate in the centre of the far edge. Go through and turn left to reach a gate on to a road. Turn right and follow the road, soon reaching, on the left, the road for the car park/picnic area.

POINTS OF INTEREST:

Eggardon Hill – The view from the hill top is exceptional, taking in the coast to Golden Cap and looking north to the hills of central Dorset. The hill fort itself is equally impressive, being smaller, but more spectacularly positioned than Maiden Castle.

Bell Stone – The steep spur edge of Eggardon Hill has seen several landslides which have caused rocks to fall to the spur's base. These have been clearly arranged into a semi-circle around the large Bell Stone, probably by Neolithic or Bronze Age folk though the purpose is obscure.

Powerstock Common – There has been a forest here since ancient times – it is known that the Saxon King Athelston hunted here. King John made it a Royal Forest and built a hunting lodge on the site of the Norman motte and bailey castle at nearby Powerstock

REFRESHMENTS:

None on route, but the start point is mid-way between *The Spyway Inn*, Spyway and the *Old Swan Inn*, Toller Porcorum.

Walk 63 **WYNFORD EAGLE** 6m (9^1/$_2$km)

Maps: OS Sheets Landranger 194; Pathfinder 1317.

On the downs above the Frome Valley.

Start: At 582960, Wynford Eagle Church.

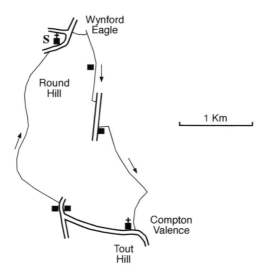

From the church go back to the village cross-roads and straight over on to a track which heads uphill, eastwards. At a track junction, turn right and follow a track with a hedge to your left. Follow the track past a barn. Continue ahead, across a field, where the track goes left, to go through a fence gap. Turn left and walk to a road (Greenford Lane). Turn right along the road to reach a pair of gates, on the left, just before a barn, also on the left. Go through the left-hand gate and cross the field beyond, keeping to the right-hand hedge. Where the hedge ends, turn right and walk to a gate near a small copse on the right. Go through and maintain direction to reach another gate beyond the brow of the shallow hill in front.

Go through, and soon go left through another gate. Now go downhill, following the right edge of a field to reach a gate. Go through, bear left through another gate and cross a field to a gate on to a track. Turn right along the track to reach a road in

Compton Valence. Turn right, passing the church and continuing up the road to reach a T-junction. Turn right, go past some farm buildings and turn left through a gate on to a bridleway along the right edge of a field. In the next field, bear right to go along its right edge. In the next field bear right and go along the right edge to reach a gate. Go through and turn sharp left through another gate on to a track. Follow the track to a gate, go through and bear right along the field edge to reach another gate, on the right.

Go through, turn left through another gate and follow a track to reach a road. Turn right along the road to return to **Wynford Eagle**.

POINTS OF INTEREST:

Compton Valence – The village is beautifully positioned in a sheltered downland hollow. The surrounding Downs show evidence of Neolithic, Roman and medieval field systems, so this has been a favoured spot for thousands of years.

Wynford Eagle – The charming 17th-century Manor House has an eagle on its central gable, mirroring the village's name. This derives from William d'Aquila – William the Eagle – who was given the manor after the Norman conquest. A later occupant of the house was Thomas Sydenham, the father of British medicine.

REFRESHMENTS:

None on route, but available in Maiden Newton, to the north, and Winterbourne Abbas, to the south-east.

Maps: OS Sheets Landranger 183; pathfinder 1280.
Linking a fine town and an excellent park.
Start: At 638165, Sherborne Abbey.

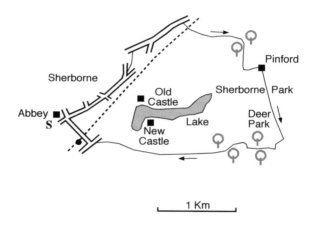

1 Km

From the **Abbey** walk eastwards to a road junction and go over into Long Street. Do not turn into East Mill Lane, to the right, continuing to the junction of several roads. Bear half-left into Oborne Road, following it to reach a track on the left by the riding stables. Follow the track to a pair of gates. Go through the right-hand one and follow the left-hand hedge in the field beyond. To the right are the ruins of Sherborne Old Castle. Go through a gate and follow the path beyond to a stile. Go over on to the A30. Turn right – there is a footpath at the roadside, but be careful – to reach St Cuthbert's Church, Oborne.

Just beyond the church, turn right through a signed gate by a cottage. Follow the path beyond, going over a stile and continuing to a gate. Go through and walk under a railway bridge to reach another gate. Go through and bear half-left, crossing a field to reach a stile. Go over, cross a plank bridge and another stile, then cross a field to a gate. Cross the field beyond to a stile into Crackmore Wood. Go over and soon turn right on a path that leads to a track. Turn left to reach a lane by the entrance gateway to Sherborne Park. Turn right through the gateway, then go first left on a track that leads through a gate, continuing to reach a stile by the house at Pinford. Go over and cross to a fence, following it (with it on your left-hand) to a footbridge. Cross the field beyond to a kissing-gate and the path beyond that as it goes uphill through the Deer Park.

Go through another kissing gate, then follow the fence on the left to a track. Turn right to reach a junction with a lane. Turn left, but very shortly turn off the lane, on to a track. Bear to the left of some barns and then follow the track through the trees to reach a kissing gate by a thatched cottage. Continue along the track to another kissing gate, following the track beyond, with views of **Sherborne Park** to the right, to reach a junction. Bear right to a kissing gate, following the path beyond to another. Go through and walk downhill to a third, going through to reach a road at a T-junction. Cross and follow the road over the railway crossing into South Street, **Sherborne**. Follow this to a junction and turn left to return to the Abbey.

POINTS OF INTEREST:

Abbey – Sherborne Abbey began as a cathedral in 705AD with St Aldhelm as its first bishop. Later there was a great Benedictine Abbey here, but it was badly damaged by fire after the priest of the town church (built after a long running dispute between the townsfolk and the monks over access to the Abbey Church) fired a flaming arrow into the wooden roof.

Sherborne Park – The old castle was built by a Norman bishop of Sherborne and destroyed during the Civil War. The new castle was built by Sir Walter Raleigh in 1594. A stone seat by the Park's lake is the reputed spot where Raleigh was doused in water by a servant who thought he was on fire as he smoked a pipe of the tobacco he had recently brought back from the New World.

Sherborne – This exquisite town is one of the finest in Dorset and well worth exploring.

REFRESHMENTS:
There are numerous possibilities in Sherborne.

Walk 65   GUSSAGE ALL SAINTS   6¹/₂m (10¹/₂km)

Maps: OS Sheets Landranger 195; Pathfinder 1281 and 1300.

An historic piece of farmland and some delightful countryside.
Start: At 994109, between Gussages All Saints and St Michael.
Park on the roadside verges near the pumping station, but please
take care not to obstruct access to utilities.

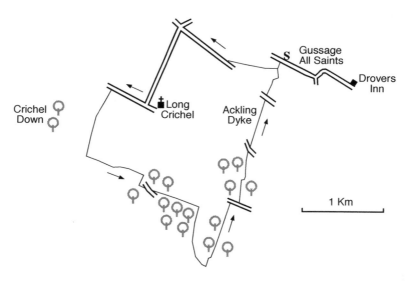

Take the path opposite the pumping station and fork right after 150 yards. The grassy
path rises easily to a stile. Go over and follow the direction of the waymarker across
a field to reach two stiles which lead to a road. Turn right and walk along this ridge
road between the valleys of the Gussage on the right and the Crichel on the left. At
a cross-roads, turn left and descend to Long Crichel. Turn right at the T-junction
and continue for about 600 yards. Now turn left on to a bridleway, go past a vehicle
barrier and walk up a long incline. Nearing the top of the rise, look right towards
Crichel Down.

About 200 yards past the highest point, make a left turn. After about ¹/₂ mile,
the track bends right to meet a road. A signpost here confirms your whereabouts. On

the other side of the road, 20 yards to the right, take a footpath which runs straight for $1/2$ mile. At the path's lowest point, turn right by a new plantation. Pass through more woodland and continue with a field on the right. Beneath an oak, a wooden seat beckons irresistibly. But... go left with the track and soon, on the left, take a small path through a gap in the hedge. The path runs behind a long row of cottages: at the far end, turn left on to a track which leads to a grassy path flanked by lightly-forested pines. The rest of the walk follows the course of the Roman Ackling Dyke (*see* Note to Walk 100). Go through some new pine plantations and across a field to reach a road. Turn right and then left on to a bridleway after less than 100 yards.

The bridleway forks right at a clear sign and drops down through spindly woods. Cross a small footbridge to reach a road and, as the road rises, bear right through a gate. The path beyond goes up a long slope to reach a road. Cross over to reach another path which descends gradually at first, then quite steeply with a dog-leg, to reach the starting point. For food and drink, take the road to the right (viewed as you return to the start), go over the bridge and up to the end of the village – just over $1/2$ mile.

POINTS OF INTEREST:
Crichel Down – The area was requisitioned during the Second World War for use as a bombing range. Post-war Whitehall bureaucrats blocked the return of the land to the owner. A subsequent cover-up led to a scandal of a 'Crichelgate' nature resulting in the resignation of the Minister of Agriculture whose department had become involved (1952-54).

REFRESHMENTS:
The Drovers Inn, Gussage All Saints.

Walk 66   **FARNHAM AND CHETTLE** $6^1/_2$m ($10^1/_2$km)
Maps: OS Sheets Landranger 184 and 195; Pathfinder 1281.
A stately home and two long barrows, linked by comfortable walking.
Start: At 958151, the road junction at Farnham.

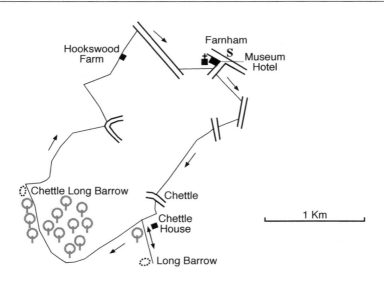

Park by the roadside and walk along the road to Chettle. Opposite the last house on the right, take a footpath on the left. Follow the path as it heads south-eastwards, in a straight line, going over stiles and across fields to reach a road by an electricity sub-station. Turn right for 100 yards and then go right again into a field. Keep to the right-hand side of the field to reach a road. Cross the road and follow a path down the left side of the fields. The path continues to a lane leading into Chettle. Turn left along the road and, very soon, turn right on a path between houses. The path goes to the right of some farm buildings and emerges opposite the church. Turn right: the entrance to **Chettle House** is immediately on the left.

    Carry on down the lane to reach a junction of many tracks. Here begins a short and interesting diversion: go through the wooden field gate and turn sharply left under huge trees. Chettle House is on the left and, further on, there are vines on the right. The bridleway dips muddily, then rises beside the **Long Barrow**. After viewing the barrow return to the track junction.

Now proceed along the next track, with a Dutch barn on your right. A few hundred yards ahead, a left wiggle brings you to an open grassy stretch. Go through a steel gate into woodland and take the left-hand track, keeping just inside the edge of the woods. Turn right at the junction at the track's end. There are small conifers on the right and, later, spiked iron railings on the left. Keep to the left when a large field is reached and at a point where small overhead wires cross your path, look left for the overgrown hump of **Chettle Long Barrow**. Follow the path around the top of a field and, at the second (waymarked) hedge gap, turn left. The path bends right and descends to reach a barn. Turn right along a track and go left where it meets a road. Now go down an ivied avenue and across the middle of a field. At a large opening in the fence, turn right on its near side and walk past the site of a late Iron Age settlement. Turn left through a metal gate and go down a, usually horse-muddy, path to reach Hookswood Farm.

Follow the farm drive up to a road and turn right. Walk down the road to a lone holly tree and turn left there, going over a stile. Cross the field beyond and go through a very small plantation. At the far corner of the next field a stile leads to the church. Turn left for the start and refreshments at the Museum Hotel.

POINTS OF INTEREST:

Chettle House – The house was built in 1710 for George Chafin, Ranger of Cranborne Chase. Its English Baroque style was the design of Thomas Archer. The gardens and some rooms are open to the public.

Long Barrow – This earthen barrow (320 feet long) dates from about 3000 BC. An opening of the barrow in about 1700 suggested the possibility of pagan Saxon intrusive burials.

Chettle Long Barrow – A shorter (190 foot) barrow than its Chettle House neighbour but of similar age. Numerous human bones were found there more than 200 years ago when part of the barrow was excavated.

REFRESHMENTS:
The Museum Hotel, Farnham.

Walk 67   ASHMORE AND TOLLARD ROYAL $6^{1}/_{2}$m ($10^{1}/_{2}$km)

Maps: OS Sheets Landranger 184; Pathfinder 1281.

A pleasant walk between two villages of striking character.

Start: At 913178, Ashmore village pond.

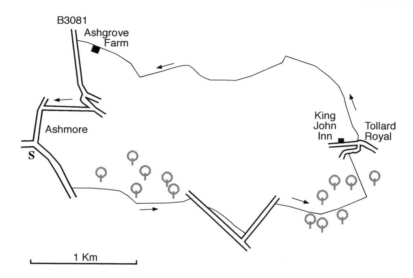

Walk down the no-through road to the south-east, and after less than $^{1}/_{2}$ mile, turn left by an area of grass. Go past some farm buildings and follow a sunken bridleway alongside a wood. Cross into Wiltshire and turn left when there is a field in front of you. The well-hooved track leads to a road: cross and continue along the track, which now runs roughly parallel to the road for nearly $^{1}/_{2}$ mile. When a side road is met, turn left along it for about 600 yards. Now, at a slight dip and a slight right bend in the road, find a stile on the right beside a field gate. The path beyond goes across a paddock, through a gate and over fences into a field. Continue in the same direction, heading for a shallow V at the far end of the field. Climb a stile near a shed into an area with woods on each side.

From the gate at the far side of this hollow, cross a field on a line to the right of a single oak tree. Next, aim for the right-hand edge of the woods ahead to reach a ladder stile followed by a mesh gate. These give access to a straight woodland path: follow it to reach a road close to Tollard church. Turn right and walk down to **Tollard Royal**, noting King John's hunting lodge on the right. As you are coming down to the pond, turn left up the road for a short distance to reach the King John Inn.

To continue the walk, take the road to the left of the pond and, very shortly, fork left up a short slope on to a green track along the valley. The track bends gently left for about $3/4$ mile and then, after a gate, drops and turns more sharply to cross the valley floor. Continue, passing a barn on the right after about $1/2$ mile, then bending into the left of two valleys and walking up to a gate. (If there are sheep about - and there usually are - dogs **must** be on leads here). After the gate, the way turns square right up the gully between two grassy hills and continues upward through Ashgrove Farm to reach a road (the B3081).

Turn left along the road. Fork right after about 500 yards and soon after turn right for **Ashmore**, leaving Wiltshire midway along the straight. It is good to hear people speaking Dorset again! At the T-junction turn left to return to the starting point.

POINTS OF INTEREST:

Tollard Royal – The village is named after the de Tollard family, landowners from Norman times. The Royal was added after a hunting lodge was built for King John. The fine Elizabethan manor house succeeded it.

Ashmore – Aisemare (the pond by the ash tree) was the Saxon name for this village which, at 718 feet (213m), is the highest in Dorset. The pond is said to date from Roman times. A midsummer festival called Filly Loo features musicians playing on a wagon from the middle of the pond, and Morris dancing.

REFRESHMENTS:
The King John, Tollard Royal.

Walk 68 MILBORNE ST ANDREW AND TOLPUDDLE $6^1/_2$m ($10^1/_2$km)
Maps: OS Sheets Landranger 194; Pathfinder 1318 and 1319.
The home of the Martyrs and their farmland. Moderate gradients.
Start: At 803976, opposite the Post Office, Milborne St Andrew.

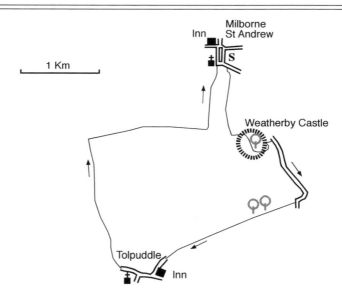

There is parking nearby at the Royal Oak (customers only) or in the village's side roads. Please be considerate to residents.

Leave the village by The Causeway, opposite the Post Office. As the road bends left, take a tiny footpath on the right. At its end, turn left, then right past farm buildings on a track signed 'Unsuitable for motors'. At a T-junction, go through the right-hand of two gates in front. Keep to the left of the field and turn left at the end by a stile and gate. In front now is **Weatherby Castle**. You are approaching it from the north-west: go up to, and round it, to the right, and keep bending left on a faint track. You will eventually find a stile to a road down below on the east side. (If you visit the top, start from the north end where an obvious track into the wood leads to the obelisk. Beyond that the way is not so clear and the ramparts are very steep – be careful.)

126

Turn right down the road. After more than $^1/_2$ mile, bend right with the road. As it turns left, go straight ahead through two farm gates and up a rising track. At the top, pick the left-hand of two gates and go up the side of the field to a small gate. Pass through a clump of oaks – and blackberries – and go along the left side of the fields beyond. A clear track leads across the next field, from which there is a view of the Piddle valley on the left. Go through a large gate, turn left and drop down to the A35 at **Tolpuddle**. The Martyrs' Inn is on the left.

Turn right on the busy road through the village, noting the green and the church. Just past the church, turn right on a stony bridleway to Dewlish. Fork right on to a grassy way which rises steadily through trees. Cross a large field, then go up the right side of two more fields (the trig. point has vanished but there is a lovely view of Dorset farmland). Start a gentle descent and, before the end of the field, drop down to the right through trees on a thin, straight path. At the end of a large field on the right, turn along its lower edge and pass some derelict buildings. In the corner, a stile and then a small gate, take you to a grassy track. Go past a barn and into a field via a Wiltshire gate. Keep to the left towards some large beech trees and turn left through a gate just past them. Turn right and walk along the side of two fields. At the end, bear right to pass triumphally between stone pillars on your return to the village, straight ahead.

POINTS OF INTEREST:
Weatherby Castle – This was an Iron Age settlement. On the tree-covered top is a brick obelisk inscribed 'EMP 1761' (for Edmond Morton Pleydell of Manor Farm, Milborne). Thomas Hardy uses this location as Ring's Hill Speer in *Two On a Tower*. The tower in the novel is based on Charborough.
Tolpuddle – On the village green, an information panel tells the story of the six local men (the Martyrs) who were transported to Australia in 1834.

REFRESHMENTS:
The Royal Oak, Milborne St Andrew.
The Martyrs' Inn, Tolpuddle.

Walk 69   **MILTON ABBAS**   6^{1}/$_{2}$m (10^{1}/$_{2}$km)

Maps: OS Sheets Landranger 194; Pathfinder 1300.

A walk from a famous village. Two short steep hills.

Start: At 809020, the top end of Milton Abbas village street. Park on the road above the school.

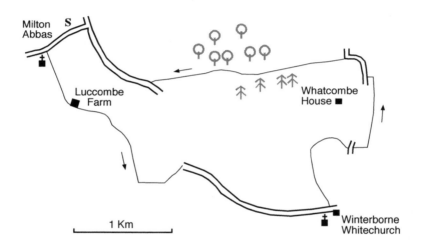

Walk down the street to St James' church and climb steeply beside it, going through a wooded belt. Cross the field over the skyline, aiming a little to the right to reach a stile in the hedge. Now cross stiles and paddocks to reach Luccombe Farm. Take the farm road up the slope, pass some buildings and turn right opposite some cottages. The track leads to a field where you keep right. Cross a stile, another field and a double stile. A few yards beyond this last stile, turn left and follow a bridleway around the field headlands to reach a road. Turn right and walk down to Winterborne Whitechurch.

Turn left between **St Mary's Church** and the Milton Arms. The road becomes a concrete farm road: where further progress is discouraged, turn right on to a stony track. **Whatcombe House** can now be seen. Cross a road and the winter bourne. Turn left after 150 yards of the slope to follow a path which, for the next ^{1}/$_{2}$ mile, is sometimes awkward underfoot. However, the park-like surroundings and the front view of Whatcombe House are adequate compensation. Turn left at a track, then right on meeting a road. Where the road bends, turn left on to a bridleway for Barnes Hill.

The way, metalled at first, becomes stony and passes a large house up on the right: continue up the narrow valley with pines on the left. Keep straight on at a vehicle barrier, going into the woods. Where the track bends noticeably to the right, bear left and soon enter a field. Now go steeply up to the left and follow the edge of a field up to a road. Turn right up the hill and, near the top, look back for a wonderful view of the Purbeck Hills and South Dorset. Turn left at a road junction to return to **Milton Abbas** and the starting point.

POINTS OF INTEREST:

St Mary's Church – The church is of 13th-century origin, though the font and pulpit date from the 15th century. John Wesley, grandfather of the Methodist leader, was vicar here during the Commonwealth years.

Whatcombe House – Like many others in this part of the county, the house is a fine example of the work of the Bastard brothers of Blandford Forum. It was built in about 1750.

Milton Abbas – The village has a street of thatched cottages that makes the Top Twelve in every English countryside calendar. The village was originally situated in the valley south of Milton Abbey, but to improve the view from his new mansion, Joseph Damer (later Lord Milton and Earl of Dorchester) acquired all the property leases by fair means and foul, relocated the village and rebuilt it in its present form (during the period 1773-80). The rebuild included the re-erection of the 16th-century almshouses opposite the church. Sir William Chambers and Lancelot 'Capability' Brown were the architects of this venture, the latter's contribution being the landscaping of the estate and the artificial lake on the site of the old village.

REFRESHMENTS:

The Milton Arms, Winterborne Whitechurch.
The Hambros Arms, Milton Abbas.

Walk 70   SPETISBURY AND THE RINGS   6¹/₂m (10¹/₂km)

Maps: OS Sheets Landranger 194 and 195; Pathfinder 1300.
Moderate walking in farmland: spring flowers and winter mud.
Start: At 916021, on a wider part of A350 in Spetisbury village
about 300 yards north-west of junction with B3075.

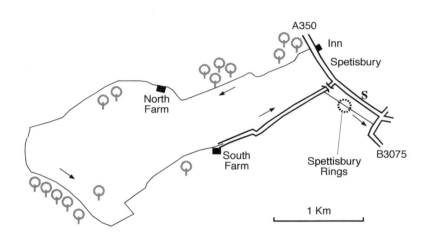

Walk up through Spetisbury for ¹/₂ mile, then turn left, almost opposite the Drax Arms,
on to a footpath to North Farm. After a few yards, go left over a stile and the field
beyond to cross a bridge over an old railway line. Keep to the right in the next field,
walking beside a wood at first. Where the wood ends, continue in the same direction,
then turn right with the power lines and follow the edge of the field past a tower. The
tower was built in the 1930's to house silage – an interesting piece of agricultural
archaeology. Carry on up the slope ahead and turn right, by a spreading beech tree,
down to North Farm.

Go through the farm and turn left. Now turn right on a bridleway after 100 yards.
Cross a field and follow a farm track with a wood on the left. Enter the long meadows
through a Wiltshire gate and go straight ahead. Bear right in the next field – passing

more agricultural archaeology in the form of a wind pump – to reach another wire gate at the far end. Go through and turn left on the crossing track. Walk up the slope, passing under some power lines, then go through a small, rusty gate to reach a junction of tracks. Take the second turning right, going along the back of a wood.

After $^1/_2$ mile or so, the track drops, then rises and becomes stony. About 100 yards past the top of the slope, turn left through a gate. Go along the side of the field beyond to the next gate. Go through and follow the track beyond up to a junction. Turn right and follow the track down to South Farm. Continue on a metalled road towards Spetisbury, but just before a railway arch, turn right into a field and take the path across **Spettisbury Rings**. From the trig. point, there is a very good view of the Rings (resembling a tilted soup plate) and of the Stour valley and Badbury Rings.

Leave the Rings from a point opposite your line of arrival, ie. at the south-east corner, where the ramparts meet the very deep railway cutting. From here, follow the path over stiles and down to a road. Turn left to reach the main road and there turn left again, with care, to complete the walk.

POINTS OF INTEREST:
Spettisbury Rings – The Rings are an Iron Age hill fort. During the building of the Somerset and Dorset railway in 1857 about 100 skeletons were unearthed. They are believed to have been the dead from a battle in Roman times. The Rings are usually spelt with a double 't', whereas the village is spelt with just one.

REFRESHMENTS:
The Drax Arms, Spetisbury.

Walk 71 MORDEN AND LYTCHETT MATRAVERS 6¹/₂m (10¹/₂km)
Maps: OS Sheets Landranger 195; Pathfinder 1319.
Undulating paths and lanes through fields and villages.
Start: At 914946, a lay-by on the west side of the B3075, adjacent
to the Cock and Bottle Inn.

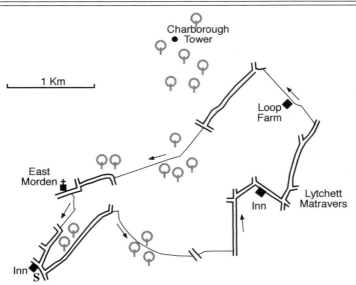

A few yards to the right, at the end of a row of cottages opposite, set off up an unmarked
road. This rises easily past a wood on the left and then a farm. Where the road bends
left, continue ahead on grass. Turn right on the nearside of a field and go downhill
beneath trees. Pass under huge power lines which, mercifully, are fairly well screened
in summer. At the lowest point, fork right over a stile and cross a usually soggy area.
Go up a bank with a small wood on the right. Work your way by stiles along the right
side of successive fields until you reach a road.

Cross the road and continue downhill in the same direction. A short, steep path
leads to a track and then to a road. Turn left and walk for ¹/₂ mile or so, ignoring two
roads going left, up to **Lytchett Matravers**. Turn right along High Street, passing
the inn (or, perhaps, not). At the cross-roads, turn left, then left again on Castle Farm

Road. About 300 yards past a turning to Loop Farm, go left over a stile opposite a nursing home. Keep right in the field and then go down through a small wood. Take the farm road which bends right into a long straight. Ahead, **Charborough Tower** is dominant. Climb a yellow stile and turn left. Walk along the road to the left for $1/2$ mile to a T-junction.

Opposite, over a stile, there is a path which parallels the power lines and pylons (known in the trade as 'towers'). Go straight ahead on entering a wood, ignoring a left fork. At a small T-junction, turn right, away from the overhead lines, keeping a field on your right. Cross a stony track by a gate and re-enter the wood briefly. Emerge on to a track again and go straight down it. Go over a stile by a steel gate and keep to the left of the field. Enter another wood over a stile, taking the path to the left which leads to a road.

Turn right and walk down to East Morden. Just before the **church**, turn left. Follow the lane as it swings right and left to arrive at a field. Turn right and then, halfway along on the right, cross by a double stile to the next field. Turn left and left again at the road to make your way back to the starting point.

POINTS OF INTEREST:

Lytchett Matravers – Named after Sir John Matravers, one of Edward II's jailers and suspected of murdering him. Sir John died in 1365 and was buried here.

Charborough Tower – Built in 1790 and rebuilt in 1839 after being struck by lightning, the tower is 120 feet high. Thomas Hardy used it as a model in his novel, *Two on a Tower*.

St Mary's Church, East Morden – Contains a kneeling statue of Sir Walter Earle (1597) whose descendent still owns nearby Charborough Park.

REFRESHMENTS:

The Cock and Bottle, Morden.

The Chequers Inn, Lytchett Matravers.

Walk 72   **SHAFTESBURY AND MOTCOMBE** $6^1/_2$m ($10^1/_2$km)
Maps: OS Sheets Landranger 183; Pathfinder 1261.
An interesting walk for its views and woodland.
Start: At 865231, the long stay car park near Coppice Street,
Shaftesbury.

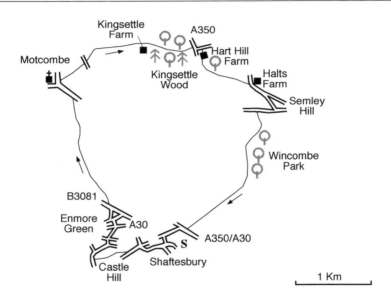

Walk along Coppice Street towards the town centre, bearing left into High Street.
Bear right (still in High Street) at the Town Hall and then turn left into Brimport. Take
the right-hand side of the road, passing **Ox House** and turning right at No 35 on to a
footpath for **Castle Hill**. Bear left to follow a metalled path to the hill's panoramic dial.
Continue ahead, going through a kissing gate and following the path beyond past the
earthworks of the old castle and down the hill. Fork left at a junction to cross rough
ground, heading for houses on Broad Lane. Turn right and follow the road. Ignore
the left turn, continuing past the old Enmore Green Methodist Church (1868). Turn
left just after, into Horseponds, and go down Well Lane. Both these roads are named
for the springs that emerged from Shaftesbury's hill. Cross the main A30, with care,

and follow the lane ahead. Go over at a cross-roads, continuing to reach the B3081. Cross, again with care, to reach, just to the right, a gate.

Go through the gate and cross the field beyond to another gate. Cross three further fields, but in the fourth turn right to follow the hedge around two sides to reach a gate to a delightful packhorse bridge. Cross and follow the left edge of a field to a footbridge. Follow the left edge of the field beyond to reach a road. Turn left into Motcombe. Bear right at the fork to reach a milestone and the village hall. Turn right on a path beside the hall (with it on your left). Cross playing fields to a gate and cross the field beyond to a gate on to a road. Cross the road and go through a gate. Follow the fence to the right to reach a gate. Turn right through it. Cross a field to a hedge gap, and the field beyond to a gate. Cross a field to reach a stile uphill of a pole.

Go over the Kingsettle Farm track to enter Kingsettle Wood, delightful mixed wood, but one through which the route can be easily lost. Essentially you are heading eastwards, using various paths to reach the main A350. Cross, with care, and take the road for Hart Hill Farm. Turn right into the stud farm, bearing left through the yard. Go through a gate and cross three fields, keeping an area of woodland to your left. Cross a field to reach a road to the right of a house. Turn right and walk past Hatts Farm. At a fork, bear right to climb steeply up Semley Hill to reach a road junction. Turn right for 200 yards, then go left along a track to a cottage. Bear right on a path beside the cottage's garden and follow it to a kissing gate at the corner of a wood. Go through and follow the wood's edge (it is on your left) to reach a stile. Go over and bear left to a gate by a barn. Follow the track beyond to a lane, bearing right along it to reach the main road. Cross, with care, and go right to reach Barton Hill, on the left. Take this, turning left into Angel Lane to regain Coppice Street.

POINTS OF INTEREST:
Ox House – This fine old Shaftesbury house is Thomas Hardy's Old Groves Place in *Jude the Obscure*.
Castle Hill – Shaftesbury was the Saxon *Sceaftesburg* meaning a fort on a promontory, an apt description for Dorset's only hill town. King Alfred fortified the hill and founded the town's abbey at the end of the 9th century. The earthworks that remain are from a later, Norman, castle. The hill's panorama dial points out the view which, on a clear day, includes Glastonbury Tor, the Quantocks and King Alfred's Tower.

REFRESHMENTS:
All tastes are catered for in Shaftesbury.

Walk 73   **THE HARDY MONUMENT**   6¹/₂m (10¹/₂km)

Maps: OS Sheets Landranger 194; Pathfinder 1332.

A walk to celebrate Dorset's other Thomas Hardy.

Start: At 602858, the church in Portesham.

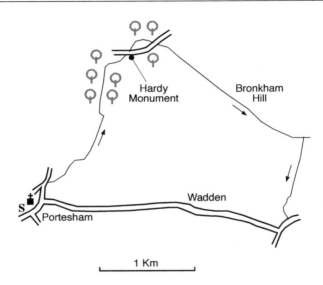

From the church head north along the village street, the road for Winterbourne Abbas, to reach a bridleway on the right signed for the Hardy Monument. Take this track to reach a gate. Go through and bear right to reach a track in the far corner. Follow a wall to a gate. Go through and walk down a field to reach another gate. Go through on to a track and turn left to walk downhill along it. Go through a gate and follow the path beyond to reach a fork. Take the left-hand branch through the woodland, bearing right at the next junction on a path signed for the Monument. Now ignore all side turnings until a signed path on the right leads to open country and the **Hardy Monument** itself.

Head north on a path to the nearby road. Cross and follow the path opposite. This bears right through bracken and heather to reach the road again. Turn left to reach a signed track, on the right, for Osmington Mills/Corton Hill. Follow this track along the ridge of Bronkham Hill, with fine views in all directions, for $1^1/_2$ miles to reach a gate. To the right here a narrow path heads south between a wall (to the left) and some rather hostile gorse bushes (to the right). Continue gingerly to reach a stile and a signpost for Corton Hill/Coryates. Go over and follow the right-hand edge of a field downhill to reach a stile on the right. Go over this and another immediately beyond, then bear left across a field to reach a track. Turn left, downhill, to reach a road. Turn right along the road, taking the first turning right towards **Portesham**. Follow this road back into the village, emerging opposite the church. For refreshment, turn left to reach the King's Arms Inn.

POINTS OF INTEREST:

Hardy Monument – Most visitors to the monument assume that it was raised to celebrate Thomas Hardy, the novelist. Since it does indeed celebrate a Thomas Hardy it can be safely assumed that some of them go away without ever realising that Dorset has two Thomas Hardys. The one celebrated here is Sir Thomas Masterman Hardy, Admiral of the Fleet, the Hardy in whose arms Nelson died at Trafalgar after saying 'Kiss Me, Hardy'. Or, perhaps, after saying 'Kismet, Hardy'. The monument, a 70 foot high octagonal tower has been described as a factory chimney, a chess pawn, a pepper mill and much worse. The very best that could be said of the work, erected in 1844, is that it is imposing.

Portesham – Admiral Hardy grew up in Portesham Manor, a fine 17th century house, its elegance being in sharp contrast to the monument. At the age of 12 he left home to become captain's boy on the *HMS Helena*, spending virtually the rest of his life at sea.

REFRESHMENTS:

The King's Arms Inn, Portesham.

Walk 74   **CORFE MULLEN**   7m (11km)

Maps: OS Sheets Landranger 195; Pathfinder 1319.

Heathland and woodland in undulating suburban Poole.

Start: At 979985, a lay-by on the north side of A31, 2 miles south-west of Wimborne Minster.

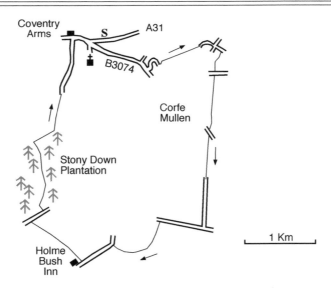

Make your way to the squat-towered **Corfe Mullen Church** and start up the B3074 beside it. Go over a bridge (over the old Poole-Blandford railway) and, after ¹/₂ mile, take the second turning left, Rectory Avenue. Follow the road around to No. 55, beside which a footpath leads to an extensive recreation area. Keep to the left side with its view of the Stour valley, Badbury Rings and Wimborne. A gate and a path lead to a new housing estate: go front left between stone posts and walk past some older houses. Cross into Pine Road and, soon, turn right at a signpost for Happy Bottom. Horseshoe signs direct you down to, and over, a bridge, beyond which the way rises slightly to reach a road where, on the right, a sign points to Upton. You are now on the line of a **Roman road**. Continue along it, ignoring all turnings. On the left you will pass a small stretch of the heathland which used to cover most of south-east Dorset before greater Bournemouth happened. Bend left with the track, turn right at an informative signpost and descend to Rushcombe Bottom. Cross Higher Blandford Road and, after some houses on the right, walk up to another small patch of heath. Keep it on your left. At the top of the ridge, opposite the playing fields, a small trace of the Roman road is discernible on the right among the brambles and bracken. Cross a road into Roman Road (!) which dips and then climbs to an unmade section. At the road ahead, turn right. After less than $1/2$ mile, turn left into Springdale Road car park. Follow the viewing point signs to their destination, being rewarded with a fine sight of Poole, its harbour and the Purbeck Hills. Go half-right towards the eyesore of industrial excavation, but about 30 yards short of the intimidating security fence, turn right and drop down through heather and gorse. A narrow path then leads to a road. Turn left.

On the near side of the Holme Bush Inn, turn right up a wide lane. At the end of this, turn right along a road. After 250 yards, turn left on a track marked 'Access Only'. This leads into Stony Down Plantation with a sign indicating private woodland - be re-assured by the blue bridleway markers. Take the main track for 200 yards, then fork left and go up through a trench. Cross the main track, twist through the trees and rejoin the track at a junction with power lines overhead. About 150 yards after this, a post marker directs you left and down into the woods. Go half-right where the ground levels and follow further waymarkers. Although these lower woods can be delightfully cool in summer, they can also be wickedly wet underfoot for much of the year. The path eventually passes green fields and reaches a road. Turn right along it and continue for $1/2$ mile via Brickyard Lane to reach the A35 where the Coventry Arms waits to refresh you. Turn right, with care, along the main road to return to the church and lay-by.

POINTS OF INTEREST:
St Hubert's Church, Corfe Mullen – The tower is from the Norman period and was restored in 1949. Inside, the wooden galleries date from about 1800. The name Mullen is said to derive from the French moulin, a mill.
Roman Road – This led from the Roman port of Hamworthy, in Poole Harbour, to Badbury Rings.

REFRESHMENTS:
The Holme Bush Inn, Upton Heath.
The Coventry Arms, Corfe Mullen North.

Walk 75　　　　**GRIMSTONE DOWN**　　　　7m (11km)

Maps: OS Sheets Landranger 194; Pathfinder 1318.

A fine hill and valley walk.

Start: At 627950, Frampton Church.

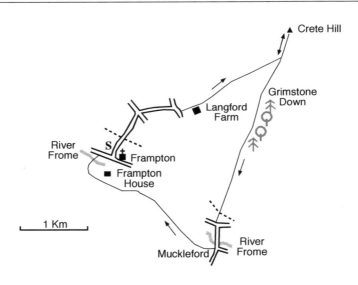

From the church head north along the minor road, crossing a railway bridge to reach a T-junction with the main A37. Cross the road, with great care, and continue along the minor road. Another road joins from the left: continue around a right-hand bend, going over a bridge (over Sydling Water, a tributary of the River Frome which is crossed twice further along the route). Now turn left along the drive to Langford Farm. Go past the farm, continuing on a track that climbs the northern flank of **Grimstone Down**, heading towards Crete Hill.

　　Go left through a gate to reach a track that is followed to the hill crest. The hill's trig. point summit is a few hundred yards to the north, but is likely to be of interest only to peak baggers as the views are just as good from the edge of the hill's plateau top. At the crest three tracks join: turn right on the one heading south towards a stand of trees. The track goes along the edge of woodland, then crosses the eastern flank of

Grimstone Down before descending into the Frome Valley. The track bears right to round a barn, then descends again to go under a railway bridge to reach the A37. To the right from here is the Royal Yeoman Inn.

Cross the main road, with great care, and take the minor road opposite. The road crosses the River Frome to reach a cross-roads. Turn right and follow a lane through Muckleford. Beyond, the quiet lane follows the line of the River Frome to reach Frampton Park. Continue along the lane to a gate. Go through this and another beyond to reach a house. Turn right here and, after about 50 yards, go left towards Frampton House. Walk past the house to reach a lane junction. Turn right and follow a lane to its junction with the A356. Turn right, with care, to return to **Frampton Church**.

POINTS OF INTEREST:

Grimstone Down – The curious ridges on the Down are the remnants of an ancient field system, probably dating from the Bronze Age as the Down also has a round barrow from that era. The track, that the walk takes along the down's eastern edge, follows a Roman road which reached the Frome Valley en route for Dorchester.

Frampton Church – The church is 17th century and has a unique west tower, an extraordinary construction financed by Robert Browne who also constructed the original Frampton House. The village itself is curious in being along the north side of the main road only. The thatched cottages that once lined the southern side were demolished to make way for trees planted, in 1840 by the then lord of the manor.

REFRESHMENTS:
The Royal Yeoman Inn, on the route.

Walk 76   EGGARDON HILL   7m (11km)

Maps: OS Sheets Landranger 194; Pathfinder 1317.

A walk with magnificent views.

Start: At 548948, the Shatcombe Lane car park, picnic area.

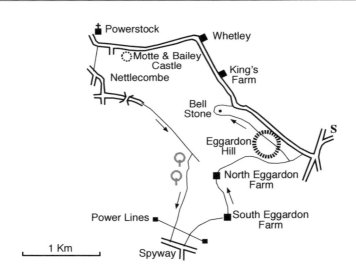

The start point lies just off the minor road that links Toller Porcorum and the A356 with Spyway, Askerswell and the A35.

From the car park, walk back to the Spyway/Toller Porcorum road and turn left. Walk down the road to a junction and turn right on to the road for Powerstock. Go along the road for 200 yards to reach a waymarked gate on the left. Head south-westward, but leave the path at the entrance to the **Eggardon Hill** fort. Go through the fort and follow a path along the steep-sided hill spur. Now scramble down the spur's steep edge to reach the Bell Stone, a Neolithic standing stone.

From the Bell Stone continue westward for 100 yards to reach a track and turn right along this, climbing over the final nose of the hill spur to reach another track. Turn right along this to reach a lane. Go left along the lane and through the hamlet of Whetely. Go past King's Farm, then beneath the slopes once topped by a Norman motte and bailey castle to reach **Powerstock**.

142

The route does not go into the village, leaving the lane to the left on a signed, enclosed path for Nettlecombe. The path runs downhill between a wall and a hedge, then crosses a footbridge. Go through a gate and bear left across the field beyond to reach another footbridge. Cross, go through a gate and head uphill towards a fence corner. Now follow the fence, with it on your left-hand, to reach a gate on to a lane at the Marquis of Lorne Inn. Turn left into Nettlecombe. Bear right at a road junction, then go left over a stile. Go through a gate and cross a field to reach a stile. Go over and walk to a gate on to a road. Turn left, following the road under an old railway bridge. Ignore the entrance to Morse Farm, on the left, continuing along the road, which soon degenerates to a track. The track can be followed to North Eggardon Farm, but a worthwhile refreshment detour goes through a signed gate on the road, heading south towards Spyway.

Follow the right field edge beyond the gate, going into a small gully to cross a stream. Continue southwards across a field to reach a gate on to a track which follows a fence, on the right. Cross a stream and walk to a gate. Go through and follow the right-hand fence to a gate on to a lane at Spyway. Turn left to reach the Spyway Inn, continuing to reach a road junction. Here, turn left through a gate to reach a track which is followed to South Eggardon Farm. There, turn left through a waymarked gate. Go through another gate, then descend to reach a sleeper bridge over a stream flowing from a pond. Go past the pond, through a gate and bear right to reach another gate. Cross a field to a gate and cross the boggy field beyond. Go across two more fields to reach a track from a house to the right. Follow this to North Eggardon Farm, turning right in front of the house. Turn left with the farm drive, then go through the gate ahead. Follow the left edge of the field beyond to reach an enclosed path. Follow the path to a gate and the track beyond that to a stile. Go over to reach the outward route below the hill fort. Now reverse the outward route back to the start.

POINTS OF INTEREST:

Eggardon Hill – The view from the hill top is exceptional, taking in the coast to Golden Cap and looking north to central Dorset. The hill fort itself is equally impressive, being smaller, but more spectacularly positioned than Maiden Castle.

Powerstock – This village of thatched cottages is the equal of any in the county. The Norman motte and bailey was used by King John as a hunting lodge.

REFRESHMENTS:
The Spyway Inn, Spyway.
The Marquis of Lorne Inn, Nettlecomb.
The Three Horse Shoes Inn, Powerstock.

Maps: OS Sheets Landranger 194; Outdoor Leisure 15.
A fascinating link between Dorset and Arabia.
Start: At 814925, the Cull-Peppers Dish car park/picnic area.

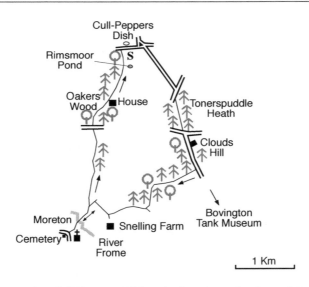

From the car park at **Cull-Peppers Dish** go back to the road and turn right along it to reach a cross-roads. Turn right and follow the road to a T-junction. Cross the road and follow the track across the edge of **Tonerspuddle Heath**. The track is indicated by blue waymarkers, though the fences of the Bovington tank training area also help to keep you on the right route. The route does change tracks twice, but each time there is a clear waymark. Follow the waymarked trail to reach a road at a T-junction. (If you do go off route on the heath, it is probable that you will reach this road to the east of the junction. If so, turn right to reach it.)

Go over and follow the road, passing **Clouds Hill** and heading towards the **Bovington Tank Museum** to reach a car park on the left. Turn right here, following a yellow waymarker along a track, keeping close to a fence on the right. Soon the track bears right to reach a waymarker post. Turn right here, going downhill on a path to reach a crossing track. Turn left and follow the track past a barrier to reach a track junction. Turn right, and right again at a T-junction. Walk to another T-junction and turn left. Soon you pass a waymarked stile on the right. The route goes over this stile, but first it goes ahead for a short detour to Moreton. Walk ahead, then bear left over a stream to reach a path fork. Take the right branch, cross a footbridge (over the River Frome) and walk into **Moreton**.

Regain the stile and go over it. Go half-right across the field beyond to reach a stile. Go over and cross a field to another stile. Go over this and another to reach a plank bridge. Cross the bridge and a stile. Go across a field to reach a similar stile/plank/stile and follow a path to reach a track near a ruin. Turn left along the track to reach a gate on to a road. Cross and follow the signed bridleway through Oakers Wood, ignoring the right turn to Oakers Wood House. Now follow the blue waymarkers going uphill through the conifer plantation on Bryants Puddle Heath to reach a track junction near Rimsmoor Pool (to the right). Go over and after about 50 yards go left on a narrow path (look out for the blue waymarkers), following it to a road. Turn right to return to the start.

POINTS OF INTEREST:

Cull-Peppers Dish – The dish is a deep, tree-lined pit across the road from the car park. It was formed by the collapse of the underlying chalk due to water percolating downwards.

Tonerspuddle Heath – This area is part of Thomas Hardy's Egdon Heath.

Clouds Hill – T E Lawrence (of Arabia) bought this cottage in 1925 when he was stationed at nearby Bovington Camp, but only began living in it in 1935. Two months after moving in he was killed in a motor-cycle accident. The cottage, which is furnished as Lawrence left it, is now a National Trust property.

Bovington Tank Museum – Just a short way south of the walk is the museum of the Royal Armoured Corps at Bovington Camp.

Moreton – The beautiful church dates from the late 18th century and has windows by Lawrence Whistler the engraver. In the cemetery across the road is the grave of T E Lawrence.

REFRESHMENTS:
The Frampton Arms, Moreton.

Walk 78   SHAFTESBURY AND DUNCLIFFE HILL   7m (11km)

Maps: OS Sheets Landranger 183; Pathfinder 1261.

An outstanding walk in north Dorset.

Start: At 865231, the long stay car park near Coppice Street, Shaftesbury.

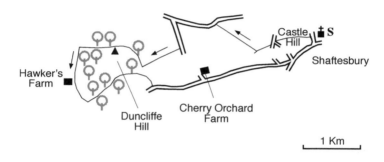

Walk along Coppice Street towards the town centre, bearing left into High Street. Bear right (still in High Street) at the Town Hall and then turn left into Brimport. Take the right-hand side of the road, passing Ox House (*see* Note to Walk 72) and turning right at No 35 on to a footpath for Castle Hill (*see* Note to Walk 72). Bear left to follow a metalled path to the hill's panorama dial. Continue ahead, going through a kissing gate and following the path beyond past the earthworks of the old castle and down the hill. Fork left at a junction to cross rough ground, heading for houses on Breach Lane. Cross the lane and bear left along the road which forms a Y-junction with it. Go past Ridge House, then turn right on to a path across Breach Common.

146

At a path junction, go right to reach a gate into a field. Keep the hedge on your left and walk to a gate on to an enclosed track. Turn right (downhill) to a gate. Maintain direction to reach a gate out of the field. Cross a field and a stream and then go uphill with a hedge on your right. Go through a gate and follow a track to the A30. Turn left along the road, with great care, for $1/2$ mile, then turn left again on a road signed for East Orchard. Go past some houses, continuing for another 100 yards to reach a path on the right. Take this, going forward to a gate and following the left-hand hedge up the hill beyond. Go into an orchard, bearing right to reach a ruin. Now go up to reach a gate into Duncliffe Wood, follow a path through it and exit via another gate to reach the trig. point summit of Duncliffe Hill.

Walk forward to reach a gate back into the wood. Stay on the path beyond, ignoring side paths and going downhill to exit the wood into a field. Follow the wood edge to a gate, on the left, going through to continue along the wood edge until you are above Hawker's Farm. Now go over a stile and cross a field to a hedge gap. Cross another field and bear left towards the southern edge of Duncliffe Wood. Re-enter the wood and bear right, uphill. Follow the track to the top of the ridge, then turn right on a path to a gate into a field. Cross the field to a bungalow and follow the track from it to a road. Turn left along the road, following it into Shaftesbury. It reaches St James Street: bear left along this, turning left after The Park into **Gold Hill**. At its top, by the **Town Museum**, turn right into High Street. Now reverse the first few yards of the route to rejoin the start.

POINTS OF INTEREST:
Gold Hill – This steep, cobbled street with its stepped cottages is Shaftesbury's most famous road and has been seen in such diverse situations as a Hovis advertisement, where it masqueraded as a northern town, and, more correctly, in the film of Thomas Hardy's *Far from the Madding Crowd*.
Town Museum – Where else in Dorset can you see a lock of Queen Victoria's hair and a dried cat?

REFRESHMENTS:
There are numerous possibilities in Shaftesbury.

Walk 79   **BULBARROW, ANSTY AND HILTON**   7¹/₂m (12km)
Maps: OS Sheets Landranger 194; Pathfinder 1299.
Beautiful hills and views, but heavy going in the lower fields in winter.
Start: At 775057, a road junction on Bulbarrow Hill.

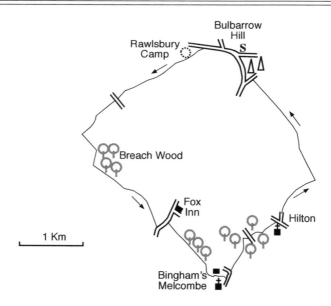

Start downhill towards Stoke Wake. After 300 yards, go through a gate on the left
– this leads to **Rawlsbury Camp**. From the top, there is a fine view of the Vale of
Blackmore and its surrounding hills. Just to the left, below the viewpoint, there is
a small gate with a Wessex Ridgeway marker. Go through it and along the rampart.
Follow the Way as it descends to a wooden gateway. In the field, go half-right – well
above the ruined buildings – to reach a gate in the far hedgerow. Cross the next field
to a waymarked gate, beyond which a narrow field funnels down to a stream. Stride
over this and, still dryshod, take a track leading to a minor road. Cross over and pass
the farm opposite.

148

Follow waymarker directions diagonally across two fields. At the far side of the next field, turn left and soon enter Breach Wood through a permanently soggy gateway. Continue along the right side of the woods. On reaching some farm buildings, turn left on a surfaced road and walk for about a mile down to habitation at Melcombe Bingham. Turn left along the road. Just before a stream, look for a stile on the right (those in need of an inn will find one 300 yards further on – but return here).

Go over the stile, which is the forerunner of two more. Continue over a footbridge and along the left side of two fields. When you reach a new plantation of broad-leaved trees, drop down slightly and fork right at a marker post. The path leads to a gate in a hedge: turn right on the park-like turf of **Bingham's Melcombe**. Follow the wall round to the front of the house and continue on grass past the **church**. Turn right over the stream and left at the road. The road very soon bends to the left: carry straight on up a steadily steepening, chalky track. Where the woods end, turn right into and across a field. Stiles on each side of a road lead to a wood through which there is a sharp descent to a gate. Keep to the left in the field down to another gate.

Ahead of you, fork left to pass **Hilton church**. Turn right on the road and then left along The Knapp. Where the lane bends left, take the track straight on. This rises, quite steeply at times, for more than $1/2$ mile. As the track turns right to a field, go left on grass through a small gate. The way (the Ice Drove) is level and true for over a mile. Hilton Bottom is below and the view of south and west Dorset goes on for ever. At the road, turn left and, shortly after, turn right to return to the starting point.

POINTS OF INTEREST:

Rawlsbury Camp – An Iron Age fort constructed in the mid-3rd century BC.

Bingham's Melcombe – An irregularly shaped 15th-century manor house. Not open to the public.

St Andrew's Church, Melcombe Horsey – Much of the church dates from the 14th century.

All Saints' Church, Hilton – Dating from the 15th century, it houses many older artefacts brought from Milton Abbey after the Dissolution.

REFRESHMENTS:

The Fox Inn, Lower Ansty (the building was once the home of the Woodhouse family. The ruins opposite are those of the original Hall and Woodhouse brewery founded in 1777. The brewery is now in Blandford).

Walk 80   HOD AND HAMBLEDON HILLS   7¹/₂m (12km)

Maps: OS Sheets Landranger 194; Pathfinder 1281 and 1300.

Steep climbs to two magnificent hill forts.

Start: At 860094, in the approach road to Stourpaine church.

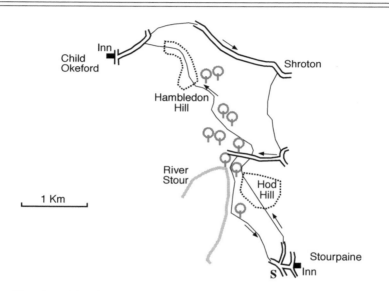

Set off northward, i.e. do not pass the church, and go straight ahead at the minor cross-roads. At the end of the village, bend left and pass some white thatched cottages. Take a bridleway to the right by a stream. There is no avoiding the long, steady pull that follows, leading to a gate and the ramparts of **Hod Hill**. Carry on by the centre path to the top and pass rectangular evidence of the Roman occupation. Follow the main path as it descends to a gate and an information board. Bear right and continue the descent to a large field gate.

    Cross the road and, slightly to the right, go up a steeply rising, chalky track. Keep to the left on entering a field. Pass woods on the left – the yew forest below is one of the largest of its kind in Europe. At a gate, turn half-right and, without losing height, cross the field to another gate. Go to the right here and turn left through a gate at the end of the field. Turn left again after 50 yards and the path takes you up to the trig. point. Continue downward beyond it.

From the first rampart of **Hambledon Hill**, head for the high ground. Go along the ridge to the right. The view from this promontory is superb – Melbury Down and Shaftesbury are front right, Duncliffe Hill is ahead, dark and isolated, and the Vale of Blackmore spreads to the left. Follow the line of the ridge as it bends left. Go steeply down on grass – be careful when it is wet – and find a thin, chalky path angling left to a gate at the left corner of a field. Here, go through ash and sycamore on a path that leads down to a road. (Turn left for the inn – 400 yards away – but return to this point.)

Turn right along the road for 150 yards and fork right on a track. After a similar distance, filter left on to a sunken, wooded path which is usually muddy. Ascend to a field with Hambledon Hill high on the right. Cross the field by a grassy track. Turn right on the road and walk for a mile to Shroton. Just past the cricket pavilion, climb a stile and go up to the left by a stone wall. An iron fence, with huge beech trees behind it, follows. At the end of the straight, go to the left of a private track where a bridleway runs beside an overgrown hedgerow. Go through two wooden gates and then turn left down the side of a field to reach a road. Turn right and soon cross your earlier route. Now turn left at a dirt lay-by just over the hilltop.

Take the second path from the right, going slightly downhill, not the path square to the right. Go through the woods on a terrace path above the River Stour. After about $1/2$ mile, the path emerges and rises on grass between hedges. Follow it all the way down, more stonily, to a sports field. Turn left for the centre of Stourpaine.

POINTS OF INTEREST:

Hod Hill – An Iron Age hill fort. In 43AD, the Durotriges Celts (Dorset people) were defeated here by Vespasian's Roman army who then occupied the fort for a short period.

Hambledon Hill – An Iron Age fort with triple ramparts. On the eastern spur there are traces of a Neolithic settlement, 4,500 years old.

REFRESHMENTS:
The Baker Arms, Child Okeford.
The White Horse, Stourpaine.

Walk 81   **SHELL BAY AND SWANAGE** $7^1/_2$m (12km)

Maps: OS Sheets Landranger 195; Outdoor Leisure 15.

A varied coastal walk of sands, cliffs and down.

Start: At 036865, the bus stop at Shell Bay café.

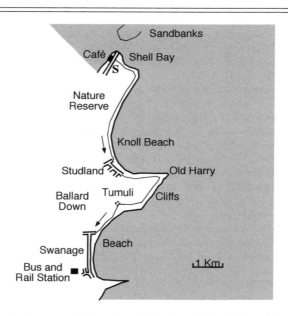

Cross the road to the seaward side and go right along the beach. Soon, there are views of **Sandbanks** and Bournemouth, and of the sand dunes of the **National Nature Reserve** on the right. At weekends and holiday times, there is also plenty of sailing as well as cross-channel ferry traffic to and from the port of Poole.

In about $^1/_4$ mile, Old Harry Rocks, Ballard Down and Studland can be seen. The next $^1/_2$ mile is a popular spot for nudists to bathe. In 2 miles the National Trust have a café, shop and toilets with Knoll car park behind. Continue along the beach until a road comes down by Middle Beach Café. Go up the road and bear left outside the Manor House Hotel. Continue on this road and turn left at the bottom of the hill, by the toilet block, on to a bridlepath. Later, follow the direction of the stone waymark 'Old Harry Rocks and Swanage'. The path goes alongside an open field by the cliff edge and through a small copse before reaching **Old Harry Rocks**, an excellent viewpoint: the shoreline of **Studland Bay**, Sandbanks, Bournemouth and beyond can be seen, as can the Isle of Wight on a clear day.

The path along the cliff edge turns sharply to the right at Ballard Point and a long steep ascent begins. In $1/2$ mile, the path divides. Take the right-hand fork and climb up Ballard Down. Swanage and Durlston Bays now come into sight. In a further $1/2$ mile, at the tumuli, keep to the path alongside the trig. point and continue climbing. After the next gate is reached, immediately turn left and start descending, following the stone waymark for Swanage.

In 50 yards go over a stile. Pass the next stile on your left and continue down the steep descent for a further $1/4$ mile. Go over a stile, and carry on towards **Swanage** for a further $1/2$ mile until a footbridge is reached. (It is possible, with difficulty, to follow the stream to the sea and to walk along the foreshore.) Cross the footbridge, ascend and cross a field, then pass between the front row of bungalows and turn left up a private road. At the top turn right and proceed into Ballard Way. At the end of the road turn left, passing All Saints Church on the right, and proceed down Ulwell Road and on to the promenade. At the end, by the Mowlem Theatre, turn up Station Road (the main street) to reach the combined bus and railway station. From here, buses will return you to the start.

POINTS OF INTEREST:
Sandbanks – The Sandbanks to Studland Chain Ferry is one of the principle routes into the Isle of Purbeck.
National Nature Reserve – Managed by the Nature Conservancy, there are walkways and hides to observe a wide variety of birds.
Studland Bay – Studland is an idyllic village. It, and the whole of the land crossed by this walk, was formerly part of the Bankes Estate, the biggest bequest ever given to the National Trust. The clean sandy beach is very popular with tourists.
Old Harry Rocks – A cluster of rocks formed by the erosion of the limestone cliffs.
Swanage – This popular seaside holiday resort was once a quarrying town. In the 19th century, George Burt supplied stone to John Mowlem in London and shipped London memorabilia back as ballast. Swanage Railway, rebuilt by volunteers, now has track as far as Corfe Castle on which steam locomotives run.

REFRESHMENTS:
Middle Beach Café, Shell Bay.
The Manor House Hotel, Studland.
The Bankes Arms Hotel, Studland.

Walk 82   **CORFE CASTLE AND SWANAGE** $7^1/_2$m (12km)

Maps: OS Sheets Landranger 195; Outdoor Leisure 15.

An exhilarating downland linear walk with magnificent views.

Start: At 959825, the National Trust car park, Corfe Castle.

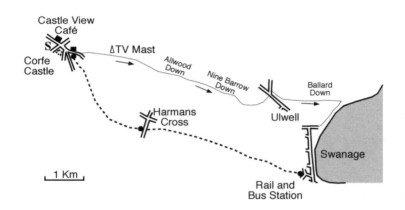

Turn left out of the car park and walk towards the village. Take the second turning on the left, Sandy Hill Lane, going under a **railway bridge** and passing Challow walkers car park (an alternative free car park and starting point). Turn left immediately through the gate signposted 'Ulwell $3^3/_4$'. The path beyond climbs steadily up the Down to its ridge. Go through the gate by the TV transmitter, beyond which an extensive view opens up northwards, of Poole Harbour, Purbeck Forest, Sandbanks and Bournemouth. Look backwards for an equally excellent view of Corfe Castle. Follow the stone waymarker for 'Ulwell $2^1/_2$' and soon Swanage appears ahead, to the right. Go through a gate on to Allwood Down – look for the stone waymarker for 'Swanage and Studland' – and pass the **tumuli** of Nine Barrow Down on the left. Stay on the ridge, following the stone waymarker for 'Ulwell $1^1/_4$'. After passing two war-time bunkers the path goes

154

through a gate and descends to the right entering the National Trust's Godlington Hill estate. From here there is a splendid view of Swanage.

Continue along the path to reach the Swanage to Studland road. Turn left and, after 50 yards, at the road junction, take the path on the right on to Ballard Down. Immediately turn right through the trees and scrub. The path contours the Down and becomes stone waymarked 'To Coast Footpath'. After $3/4$ mile, where the path is intersected by another, keep straight on. Go through a large patch of gorse to reach a junction with the coast path at the cliff edge. Turn right and go over a stile. After $1/2$ mile a footbridge is reached. Here it is possible, with a little difficulty, to follow the stream on to the beach and walk on the foreshore. The easier route crosses the footbridge, ascends and crosses a field. Pass between the front row of bungalows, turn left and then go right up a private road and proceed into Ballard Way. At the end of this short road, turn left down Ulwell Road and continue to the promenade. At the end, by the Mowlem Theatre, turn up Station Road (the town's main street) to reach the combined railway and bus station. From there return to the start by taking the steam train or Nos. 142 or 143 buses (which run hourly) back to Corfe Castle.

POINTS OF INTEREST:

Railway bridge – The Swanage Railway ran between Swanage and Furzebrook. The line was dismantled during the Beeching era, but in the early 1970s the Swanage Railway Co. Ltd. was formed to relay the track and run steam trains along it. The track currently extends to Corfe Castle. The railway, run by volunteers, offers a regular service at weekends and throughout the week in high summer. The trains are drawn by restored steam locomotives.

Tumuli – The tumuli on Nine Barrow Down are Bronze Age round barrows.

REFRESHMENTS:

The National Trust Castle View Café, Corfe Castle.

The National Trust Tearooms, Corfe Castle.

There are also other possibilities in Corfe Castle and a wide selection of inns and cafés in Swanage.

Walk 83   KIMMERIDGE AND TYNEHAM $7^1/_2$m (12km)

Maps: OS Sheets Landranger 194 and 195; Outdoor Leisure 15.

A spectacular ridge and cliff walk.

Start: At 918801, the Quarry car park above Kimmeridge.

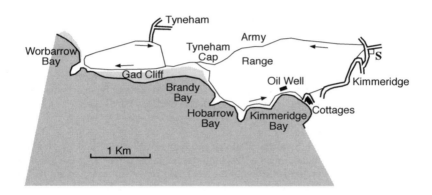

Warning: This walk is over the MOD Lulworth Range. This is generally open at weekends and throughout August. However, it is imperative that walkers check to ensure the range is open and that, for their own safety, they keep between the yellow markers.

Leave the car park and turn right to the road junction. Go over and cross the second stile on the left. Follow the path beyond, signposted 'Range Walks 1 Steeple Leaze 1', along the ridge, with Kimmeridge Bay and the **Clavel Tower** seen below and to the left.

Enter the Lulworth Range through a kissing gate. The path is well-defined by yellow marker posts and a stone waymarker for 'Worbarrow Bay $1^3/_4$'. Keeping to the ridge the path goes over Tyneham Cap and Gad Cliff before descending steeply into Worbarrow Bay. From here, there are fine coastal views westward, as far as Portland.

Go over a stile and after 30 yards turn inland and follow a track up the valley bottom for $^2/_3$ mile to reach Tyneham. Turn left at the top and go past the car park into the remains of **Tyneham** village. Return to the top of the track from Worbarrow Bay and go over the stile. Now follow the path up the hill side – there is a stone waymarker for 'Kimmeridge $1^3/_4$' – keeping between the yellow marker posts. At the top (Gad Cliff), turn left along the cliff. Shortly, go over a stile and take the right-hand path stone waymarked for 'Coast Path – Kimmeridge Bay' which contours Tyneham Cap and then descends to follow the cliff edge above Brandy and Hobarrow Bays.

Leave the Lulworth Range through the heavy steel gates. Walk past **BP's Kimmeridge Well site** with its nodding donkey pump and continue past the row of cottages at Gaulter Gap. At the public toilet block, go over the stile opposite and strike diagonally across the field beyond to reach another stile on the right. Go over and cross the field beyond to reach a further stile. Go over and turn left along the road beyond which leads up to **Kimmeridge** village. At the top of the village go through gates into the churchyard and follow a path to the right. Go through a kissing gate and climb straight up the steep field beyond. At the top, go over a stile and turn right. The car park is now just 50 yards away.

POINTS OF INTEREST:

Clavel Tower – The tower is a now-dangerous ruin built in 1820 by the Rev Richards of Kimmeridge and named for the Clavel family from whom the vicar had descended. Its purpose is unknown: probably it was just a folly.

Tyneham – This village and the land surrounding it was commandeered by the War Department in 1943 as a training ground for Allied Forces. The village has never been returned to its rightful owners. The village church and schoolroom are open to the public: there is an exhibition in the church and the schoolroom is set out with 1960s desks on which there are exhibits of pupils work.

Because the land around the village of Tyneham has not been worked, the flora and fauna has been preserved from the ravages of modern farming methods.

BP's Kimmeridge Well Site – BP drilled its first borehole in 1937 and is currently extracting 3,500 gallons of oil per day.

Kimmeridge – This attractive village of stone and thatch is part of the Smedmore Estate which has been in the Clavel (and then Mansel by marriage) family for over 500 years.

REFRESHMENTS:

None on the route, but the Kimmeridge Post Office offers a limited range.

Walk 84   LONGBURTON $7^1/_2$m (12km)

Maps: OS Sheets Landranger 183 and 194; Pathfinder 1280.
A walk through the pastoral elegance of the Blackmoor Vale.
Start: At 649128, the church in Longburton.

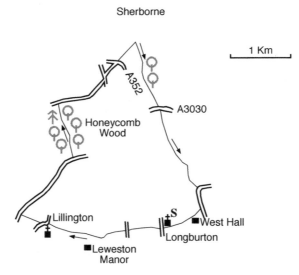

From the church walk down to the main road (the A352) which bisects the village.
Cross this, with great care, to reach a farm drive. In the farmyard, go over a stile and
follow an enclosed path (between a hedge and a wall). Cross two fields, using gates
to go between them, to reach a gate, in the second, on to a road. Cross straight over
and follow a path into woodland. Go over a stile and cross a field to reach a gate to
a road. Turn left to a cross-roads. To the right here is a kissing gate: go through and
cross to a gate. Go through this and walk ahead to cross a stile. To the left here is
Leweston Manor.

Keep to the right of the farm buildings, following the track towards Lillington
Church, seen ahead. Go over a stile to the right of the church and walk down to the
road in **Lillington** village. Turn left then, where the road bears left, turn right through
a gate. Follow the track beyond to a road. Turn right along the road to reach the edge

of Honeycomb Wood (after a walk of about 1 mile), to the left. Continue for about 30 yards to reach a gate, on the left, into the wood. Follow the track in the wood, soon reaching a fork. Take the left-hand branch which rises steadily to a ridge. Soon after starting a descent from the ridge, a path goes off to the left: take this, heading downhill to reach a junction of paths.

Turn left, heading uphill for about 100 yards to reach a path, to the right, that heads downhill through beautiful oak trees. Cross a side track and go through an obvious gap into a field. Cross the field to reach a stile in its right-hand corner. Go over to reach a short flight of steps down to a road. Turn right along the road for about $3/4$ mile. A track comes in from the right at a left bend: stay with the road to reach a right turn (signed for Longburton) a few yards further on. Take this right turn to reach the A352. Go straight across, with great care, into the 'No Through Road'. Go past playing fields, then turn right, at a house, on to a path that runs between railings and a field edge. Continue uphill along a **track** through woodland. Go over a ridge and descend to reach a main road (the A3030). Go over, with care, to reach two gates. One leads into a field: go through the other which leads to a continuation of the old track into the **Blackmoor Vale**.

Follow the track to a road. Turn right for 200 yards, then go right again along a drive (signed as a 'Private Drive' – but do not worry it is a right of way). To the left here is West Hall, a 15th-century (but much modified) mansion. Follow the drive back to Longburton: from its end it is just a short step back to the starting point.

POINTS OF INTEREST:

Leweston Manor – This old manor house is now a school. The chapel is 17th century, the church much more modern.

Lillington – The village church dates from the 12th century, the barn beside it, a magnificent building, from the late 16th century.

Track – This old track was the main, indeed the only, road from Sherborne to Dorchester before the turnpike road – now the A352 which goes through the starting village of Longburton – was built.

Blackmoor Vale – In Hardy's novels this is the 'Vale of Little Dairies'.

REFRESHMENTS:

The Rose and Crown Inn, Longburton.

Maps: OS Sheets Landranger 183 and 194; Pathfinder 1280.
A walk along the River Stow.
Start: At 787161, Hinton St Mary Church.

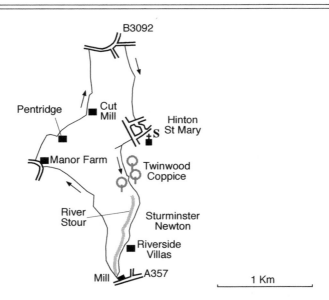

Go back to the village road (and the White Horse Inn) and turn left to reach the B3092.
Cross straight over into a lane and follow it to where it bends right. Here, to the left,
there are two gates. Go through the first of these (the left-hand as you face them) and
follow a hedged path to a field. Beyond this, walk with the fine woodland of Twinwood
Coppice on your left to reach a section of the wood that crosses your path. Go through
this to reach a stile. Go over this and another a short distance further on to reach the
River Stour. The walk now continues with the river to the right and the houses of
Sturminster Newton to the left: head for the left end of an old railway bridge, crossing
a stile and going under the bridge to reach a line of trees. Keep these on your left, but
look through them to spot **Riverside Villas**, the last building passed.

Go through a kissing gate and turn right. Go uphill slightly to reach a gate into a
recreation ground. Follow the trees to an exit gate and head for Sturminster Newton

Mill, visible ahead. Go over a stile and a bridge (close to the Mill), and turn right. Go over a stile and head for a house, crossing a stile there on to a lane. Turn right along the lane, following it for about a mile to reach Blackwater Bridge over the River Divelish. In its last yards to the bridge the lane degenerates into a muddy track, but is easily followed.

Follow the path beyond the bridge to reach a metalled lane, and follow the lane to a road at Manor Farm. Go right, then right again on a lane signed for Bagber Manor Farm. Cross a bridge over the old railway. Beyond this the lane turns sharply right and continues to a gate. Ahead is **Pentridge Farm**. The route does not, however, go through the gate or visit Pentridge. Instead, it goes left, off the lane, on a track between a house and a metal barn. Go through a gate and head towards a thatched house. Cross a stile in a field corner, go through a gate on the left and follow a ditch (to your right) to reach a bridge over the River Stour. Cross to reach **Cut Mill**.

Go over a stile on the left and follow the Stour's bank to another stile. Bear half-right across a field, then go right through a hedge gap. Turn left and go over a pair of stiles. Cross a field to another stile. Go over, walk past a pond (to the left), go over another stile and follow the track beyond to a road. Turn right to the road's junction with the B3092. Go left along this road, then almost immediately right on a minor road. Follow this for 150 yards, then go right through a gate. Follow the left-hand hedge of the field beyond to reach a footbridge. Cross this and the next field to reach another bridge. Cross and follow a path towards trees. Keep these on your right-hand to reach a track and follow it to reach a road in **Hinton St Mary**. Go right, then immediately left to reach a T-junction. Turn right to return to the church.

POINTS OF INTEREST:

Riverside Villas – The left-hand house was where Thomas Hardy lived for the first two years of his married life, from 1876 to 1878. He wrote *The Return of the Native* in the house.

Pentridge Farm – The famous Dorset dialect poet William Barnes, the mentor of Thomas Hardy, was born here.

Cut Mill – This corn mill was built in the 18th century and, with its water wheel, is a delight.

Hinton St Mary – The remains of a 4th-century Roman villa show that Hinton has been a favoured site for centuries. The church has a medieval tower, but was substantially rebuilt in 1846. Inside there is a fine 12th century font.

REFRESHMENTS:
The White Horse Inn, Hinton St Mary.

Walk 86   **ANCIENT DORSET**   7$^1/_2$m (12km)

Maps: OS Sheets Landranger 194; Pathfinder 1317 and 1331.

A walk past some of the most ancient sites in Dorset.

Start: At 588859, the Bishop's Limekiln Picnic Area.

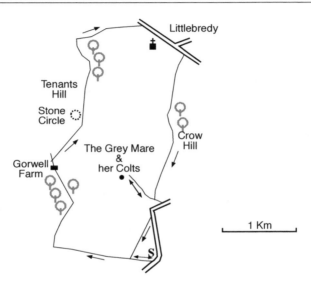

The picnic area/car park is reached by taking the minor road for the Hardy Monument and Winterbourne Abbas from Abbotsbury.

From the site, go back on to the road and turn left, uphill. Almost immediately, go left again along a track. Ignore a track on the right (the return route arrives here) and a gate on the left, continuing to reach a gate and stile. Go through or over to reach a track fork. Take the left-hand branch, but leave it soon after, heading half-left across a field to reach a stile. Go over and follow the fence on the left to reach a track. Turn right along this. Ignore a turning to the left, maintaining direction to reach a gate. Go through, cross over at a track junction and walk to a gate beside a barn. Go through to a Y-junction. Bear right on the track for White Hill. Go uphill to reach three gates. Go over the stile beside the centre one and follow a track beside a fence (on your left) to a T-junction. Turn right and follow it as it bears left to a gate. Go through and continue along the track to reach a gate on to a lane. Turn left, following the lane through woodland to reach Gorwell Farm. Go past the farmhouse, to the left, and ignore turns to the right and the left to reach a gate. Go through and turn right along a fence. Maintain direction where the fence ends, going through several fields, linked by gates, to reach the **Kingston Russell Stone Circle**, to the left.

From the circle head north along the edge of a small copse, then bear half-left across Tenants Hill to reach a bridleway heading north. This descends along the edge of a wood, then bears half-left to a hedge gap. Go half-right in the field beyond to reach a gate in its right edge. Go through, crossing a stream, several fields (linked by gates) and another stream to reach a gate on to a road. Turn right and follow the road through Littlebredy. Bear right at a road fork to reach the village cricket pitch, to the right. Here a signed bridleway goes right, following the pitch's edge to a gate. Go through and climb up the hill ahead. At the top, aim for the copse on Crow Hill, going along its right (western) side to reach a gate. Go through and continue southwards, with a view to the left of the Hardy Monument. The sign warning of low-flying aircraft refers to models, though it should still be heeded. At a distinct left bend, go through the gate on the right for a short detour to visit **the Grey Mare and her Colts**. The detour adds a total of about $1/2$ mile to the walk. Return to the track and follow it to a road. Turn right. The road soon bends sharply left: go through the gate ahead on to a track signed for West Bexington, soon leaving it, to the left, to reach a signpost for Abbotsbury. There, go half-right on a track that reaches a gate. Go through and follow a track to reach the outward route. Turn left to return to the start.

POINTS OF INTEREST:
Kingston Russell Stone Circle – This fine Bronze Age stone circle consists of 18 stones and dates from about 2000 BC.
The Grey Mare and her Colts – This evocatively named site is actually the remains of a Neolithic long barrow.

REFRESHMENTS:
None on the route, but available at nearby Abbotsbury and Portesham.

Walk 87   DURDLE DOOR AND BURNING CLIFF $7^1/_2$m (12km)
Maps: OS Sheets Landranger 194; Pathfinder 1332 and Outdoor
Leisure 15.

A fine coastal walk with a Downland return.
Start: At 811804, the car park near Durdle Door.

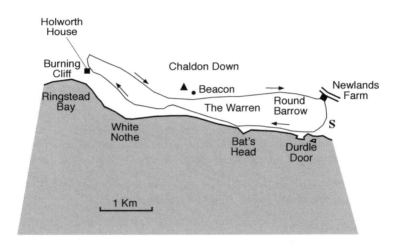

To reach the start take the minor road from Winfrith Newburgh (a village just off the
A352) towards West Lulworth. At Newlands Farm, where the road turns sharply left,
take the road towards the sea. The car park is near the end of this road.

From the car park take the signed path for Durdle Door, going steeply down
to the cliff edge above Man o' War Bay. Bear right along the cliff to **Durdle Door**.
Continue along the cliff path (which is part of the Dorset Coastal Path) going steeply
up and over Swyre Head and descending to reach **Bat's Head**. Westward the path
rises and falls along the cliffs below The Warren to reach White Nothe, a beautiful
viewpoint into Ringstead Bay. Continue westwards to reach Holsworth House and
Burning Cliff.

164

Beyond the house a path leaves the Coastal Path to the right. Take this, going inland to reach a path junction. Turn right here on to a fine downland path that passes several Bronze Age round barrows. Beyond, the path goes south of the high point of Chalden Down and a prominent Beacon, then bears left, away from the sea, to reach another round barrow, this one topped by a Lowthorn tree. Just beyond the barrow the path forks: take the right branch and follow it to reach a track that continues to Newlands Farm. Now turn right on the road used to reach the car park, following it back to the start.

POINTS OF INTEREST:

Durdle Door – A continuation of the twisted rock strata and non-stop battering by the sea has created a beautiful rock arch. Understandably it is one of Dorset's most photographed features.

Bat's Head – One day the rock arch of Durdle Door will fall, but a replacement, though smaller, is being created here.

Burning Cliff – The cliff gets its name from two occasions in the 1820s when it caught fire, pouring oily black smoke into the sky. The smoke came from the ignited bituminous shale of which part of the cliff is formed. It was ignited by rapid oxidation of iron pyrites. The cliffs between Burning Cliff and White Nothe were the escape route for smugglers in J Meade Falkner's classic book *Moonfleet*.

REFRESHMENTS:

None on route, but readily available in nearby West Lulworth.

Walk 88   **BURTON BRADSTOCK** $7^{1}/_{2}$m (12km)

Maps: OS Sheets Landranger 193 and 194; Pathfinder 1317.

An interesting walk to a misnamed village.

Start: At 489895, Burton Bradstock Church.

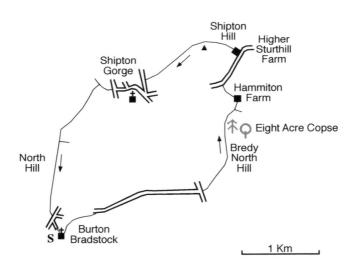

From the church walk down Darby Lane and turn right into Grove Road. Follow the road to its end, near a watermill. Follow the path, which at first lies beside the River Bride, then leaves it, going left to reach a road. Turn right along the road, passing Graston Farm, to the right and continuing to a T-junction. Go straight over and follow a farm track for about 300 yards to reach a gate and stile on the left. Go over and turn right to go through a gate. Turn left and follow a bridleway up Bredy North Hill, staying to the left of a clump of trees (Eight Acre Copse). Continue along the bridleway to reach a lane. Turn left, passing through Hammiton Farm and continuing to reach a road.

Turn right along the road to reach a bridleway to the left. Follow this through Higher Sturthill Farm and on up **Shipton Hill**, turning left near the top to reach its trig. point summit. Cross the summit and descend to reach a footpath heading south-west.

166

Follow this down to reach a road. Turn left and walk to a cross-roads, turning right there into **Shipton Gorge**. Walk past the church, then bear left to follow the road to a T-junction. Go straight over, following a track that heads due west for 100 yards to reach a gate on the left. Follow the left-hand hedge to reach a stile. Go over and follow a path across several fields linked by stiles to reach a crossing track. Turn left and follow the track to a sharp left bend. Here go straight ahead through a waymarked gate and follow a bridleway up and over the eastern shoulder of North Hill. Now descend the bridleway to reach a road in **Burton Bradstock**. Turn right, then take the first turning left and follow the road back to the church.

POINTS OF INTEREST:

Shipton Hill – This distinctive, conical hill was used as a landmark by fishermen operating off Chesil Beach. As might be expected, it is topped by an Iron Age hill fort.

Shipton Gorge – Many visitors are fooled by the village's name, which has nothing to do with any geological feature. It derives from the Norman family of de Gorges who were given the manor after the invasion of 1066.

Burton Bradstock – Burton is a very pretty place set close to where the River Bride reaches the sea. Its narrow lanes are a joy to explore, as is St Mary's Church. The 15th-century building houses a clock brought here from Christ's Hospital in London. The Drove Inn was once a smuggler's inn, Isaac Gulliver, Dorset's most notorious smuggler, using it as the centre for his operations.

REFRESHMENTS:

The Drove Inn, Burton Bradstock.
There are also other possibilities in Burton Bradstock.

Walk 89　　MELBURY PARK AND LEWCOMBE　　8m (13km)

Maps: OS Sheets Landranger 194; Pathfinder 1298.

A sometimes difficult, but very worthwhile walk through Melbury Park.

Start: At 573045, Evershot Church.

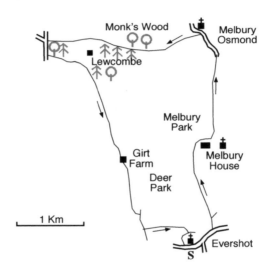

Walk along the village street towards Holywell, ignoring a turning to the right (for Maiden Newton) to reach the drive, to the left, for Melbury Park. Go between the lion-tamed gate posts. After a few yards go ahead at a fork to walk through the park. Go through a kissing gate and walk to the rear of **Melbury House**, bearing right to walk alongside it. Now go with the entrance drive as it turns left and heads northwards, following it through three gates to the end of the road in **Melbury Osmond**. Go through the village, but before reaching the church turn left up a lane opposite Rock Cottage.

Follow the lane to a gate where a track joins. Go through and follow the track across several fields, aiming for the woodland ahead. Keep the wood edge on your left hand to reach a gate in the left corner of a field. Go through and turn right on a path that can be very boggy after rain and follow it to a bridge over a stream. Lewcombe, the next point on the walk, is just to the left now, but there is no right of way directly to it, so go forward, crossing a field to reach a gate. (Do not turn right through a gate, but walk ahead to reach one that is hidden from view.) Go through and cross a field to a road. Turn left.

After 200 yards go left again along the drive to Lewcombe House. Go past a cottage, on the right, to reach a stile, also on the right. To visit the House and its church continue along the drive. The walk goes over the stile and bears right across a field to a gate. Go through and cross the next field to reach a stile. Go over, cross a river (it is forded and so can be difficult after heavy rain) and climb steeply up its far bank to reach a field. Cross this field close to its left edge to reach a gate. Go through and cross several smaller fields to reach a track. Bear left with this to reach Girt Farm. Go through the farmyard and bear left on to the farm drive. Follow the drive along the edge of Melbury Park to reach a distinctive right turn. Stay with the lane around this, but soon look to the left to find a stile into a field. Follow the left hedge, go through a gate and cross the field beyond to a stile on to a lane. (Dirty Lane?!). Cross the lane into a field and follow its edge, bearing right with it to reach a gate on to a lane in **Evershot**. Turn right and follow the lane around a left turn to reach a road. Turn left to return to the church.

POINTS OF INTEREST:

Melbury House – This huge house was built in the 16th century by the Strangways family, but has been modified and enlarged several times since. The hexagonal tower is original. Its purpose is not known, but most experts think that it was an observation tower for the deer park, believing that senior members of the Strangways family watched the hunting from it. The nearby chapel is older than the present house, dating from the 15th century. It has a collection of interesting memorials to the Strangways family including two alabaster effigies of knights in full armour.

Melbury Osmond – With its array of thatched cottages this is one of the prettiest villages in Dorset. In the church Thomas Hardy's mother and father were married in 1839. Sadly 50 years after the wedding the restorers were let loose. The couple would hardly recognise the place now.

Evershot – Evershot is beautifully positioned on a hill site that makes it one of Dorset's highest villages. The village inn, the *Acorn*, is the *Sow and Acorn* of Thomas Hardy's *Tess of the d'Urbervilles*. The link between the book and Tess' Cottage, opposite the church, is more tenuous.

REFRESHMENTS:
The Acorn Inn, Evershot.

Walk 90 WILTSHIRE BORDER AND THE OX DROVE $8^1/_2$m ($13^1/_2$km)
Maps: OS Sheets Landranger 184; Pathfinder 1261, 1262, 1281 and 1282.

A woodland reserve and views in neighbouring Wiltshire.
Start: At 003195, the car park at Garston Wood, two miles north of Sixpenny Handley on the road to Bowerchalke.

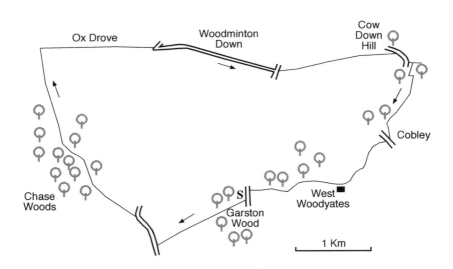

From the car park set out westward, going slightly uphill into the coppices of **Garston Wood Nature Reserve**. Go over a stile, then pass a low barrier and enter a field. Cross this, maintaining direction and start descending with a hedge on the left. Go into the left of two fields and keep to the right to reach a gate in the corner. Go through and down to a road. Turn right and follow the road for $^1/_2$ mile to its end. Cross the unmanned frontier into friendly Wiltshire and take the track for West Chase Farm. After a few yards, at a bend, carry straight on into a wooded lane. This, by way of a narrow valley, leads to two steel gates a mile later. Go through the left gate and gain height steadily up the ridge with the enjoyment of improving views.

At the top of the slope, brick and flint barns (one, a former dwelling) welcome

170

you to the **Ox Drove**. Turn right and stride out, walking 'on top, top of the world'. The view on the left is across the Ebble Valley. Continue on the same line when you join a road and before long most of South Wiltshire appears panoramically on the left. At a T-junction, go across on to a rutted, grassy track. Another mile brings you to a barn and a stand of majestic beeches. Here turn right along a road. After about 200 yards, where the road turns right, turn left along a track. Within 50 yards, turn right into the wood on a faint path, best recognised by a yellow waymarker on the old oak tree, returning to the home county.

Pass under or by toppled trees for about 300 yards until a stile gives access to a field. Keep to the left to reach a gate in the far corner. Go through and take the tree-lined track beyond. As the track approaches Cobley, turn left through a gate and keep to the right of a field. At its end, go through two gates and cross a narrow road to reach a small wooden gate in the hedge, a little to the right. With Pentridge Hill keeping watch on the left, walk along the hedge and into the next field, a very large one. Go down the left-hand side, passing West Woodyates, its cottages and a pond. Continue along the same track, passing a wood on the right, until it bends to the left through a belt of woodland. Turn right behind the woodland and walk up the side of a field. At the road, turn left to return to the car park.

POINTS OF INTEREST:
Garston Wood Nature Reserve – The Reserve is especially attractive in springtime with its primroses and bluebells, but has much to offer throughout the year having a wealth of native flora and fauna. In addition, the ancient art of coppicing is practised here. Descriptive leaflets are available at the site.
Ox Drove – The drove is one of the ancient trackways through Cranborne Chase. Despite its name, it was mostly used for the movement of sheep in the centuries before motor transport.

REFRESHMENTS:
Unfortunately, there is nothing available on the route, but there are two inns – *The Star* and *The Roebuck* – at Sixpenny Handley, two miles south of the car park.

Walk 91   **FONTMELL MAGNA AND ASHMORE** $8^1/_2$m ($13^1/_2$km)
Maps: OS Sheets Landranger 183 and 184; Pathfinder 1281.
Views - and hills - to take one's breath away.
Start: At 867168, the Crown Inn, Fontmell Magna.

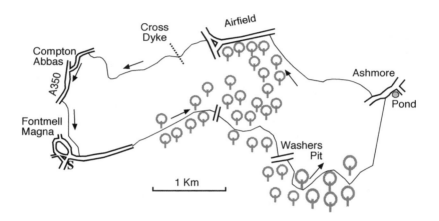

Leave the village by the road opposite the Crown Inn, beside the garage, and after $^1/_2$ mile, just past the Springhead pool, fork left as the road bends right. The straight track leads to a steep rise through some woods. Continue uphill on grass to reach the reward of a short, flat stretch above the valley. On the flat, fork right and upwards again to reach a waymarked wooden gate into more woods. Go up through the woods to reach an open space. There, turn right to walk alongside a new plantation to reach a road. Cross and go into the woods opposite, proceeding down the main track. About 200 yards past the end of a field on the right, turn left and then immediately right. The track descends, goes straight across at a junction, passes some observation steps and then drops steeply through the trees to meet a main bridleway. Turn right and follow this, bending right at the valley bottom and continuing to reach a road at Washers Pit. Turn left for 100 yards, then, to the left of the Forestry Commission gate, take a

172

path going steeply uphill. There were alterations to certain rights of way in the next $1/2$ mile of route in December 1993 so they may not appear on your map. At the top of the slope, bend right with the track and then soon fork left. After 200 yards, turn left on a prominent bridleway which before long runs up the side of woods which are at their best at bluebell time. Go past a field on the left and, after a right bend, go past another. Now go past a disintegrating hut and walk downhill. Turn left just after a grassy dip and, shortly, leave the woods to go up the side of a field. Turn left on a wide farm track for about $1/2$ mile to reach a road. Turn right for 150 yards to reach Ashmore pond (*see* Note to Walk 67).

Retrace your steps, but stay on the road and then turn right after the last of the farm buildings (there is a blue arrow waymarker). The path passes the farm and drops down the right side of a field to reach Shepherds Bottom. In these parts, the ups are Downs and the downs are Bottoms!. Go left, up the slope, and through gates and fields to reach the corner of West Wood. Keep the wood on your left to reach a road. Turn left and walk alongside Compton Abbas airfield for $1/2$ mile, then fork right at a road triangle to cross a busy road, with care, on to **Fontmell Down**. Walk along the ridge and through the Cross Dyke. Bear right immediately to cross a stile, then turn left and maintain height for about 400 yards. From here, a terrace track soon descends steeply: at a wooden gate, go down and right to a stile between two gates. The path beyond leads to a covered lane which is followed towards Compton Abbas. Turn left at a narrow road and left again at the A350. Walk carefully along the main road for about 500 yards, escaping over a stile on the left, just past the entrance to Manor Farm. Go around the cricket field to the left corner where a damp thicket hides a stile into the next field. Keep to the right of this field at first, but then ease left to find a cattle bridge over the stream at its end. Cross another field to reach a stile to the left of a Dutch barn. Go half-left after this to a stile in the corner of a field. Go over and turn right down the road back to **Fontmell Magna** and the Crown Inn.

POINTS OF INTEREST:

Fontmell Down – This is National Trust land with wonderful views over Blackmore Vale. The Cross Dyke is one of many examples on the Wessex chalk downs. It is believed to have been a territorial boundary.

Fontmell Magna – A village of great antiquity. The Domesday Book (1086) records it as Fontemale.

REFRESHMENTS:

The Crown Inn, Fontmell Magna.

Walk 92   **BULBARROW AND MILTON ABBAS** $8^1/_2$m ($13^1/_2$km)
Maps: OS Sheets Landranger 194; Pathfinder 1299 and 1300.
Some hills; outstanding views and a famous abbey and village.
Start: At 782059, the car park on Bulbarrow Hill.

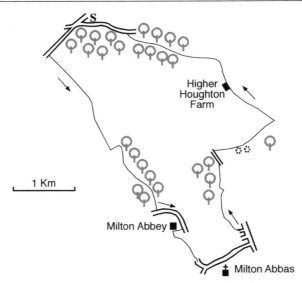

Take the road to Ansty, going past the radio mast. Now, as the road begins to drop to
the left, turn left along a track. Follow this – the Ice Drove – with a fence on the left:
the view from this ridge takes in south and west Dorset, with Nettlecombe Tout and
Ball Hill close by. Below is the gracefully sculpted Hilton Bottom – at its best when
the gorse is in flower. After about a mile, at a large hedge and a small gate, turn left
and go past an unsightly dump. Turn right and keep to the right through Green Hill
Down Nature Reserve. Another small gate leads to a lengthy descent through coppiced
woods. A final steeper drop reaches a road. In front is the glorious **Milton Abbey**, set
in a natural amphitheatre. Turn left and follow the road past the main drive to reach
a second (public) entrance on the right. Observe carefully the directions to the abbey
and grounds. Leave the abbey grounds by the Lake Lodge path to the south-east – it is
the only right of way – which is fenced and runs close to water meadows and then to

174

the lake. At the lodge, turn right along a road, then go left up through Milton Abbas. Walk the full length of the village street: the tea shop and inn are both on the right.

Turn left at the top of the street and take the second turning left. Go through a gate at the end and bear half-right across a field to another gate. Keep to the left side of the large field beyond, turning right at the end on to a stony drive. Pass a private drive on the left, but then turn by an old water trough: a grassy stretch now goes beside a wood. The route through the next field and past a shed could be difficult as the area is often a quagmire of mud and cattle slurry. Others before you have used a parallel track in the woods. Where this meets a road and the designated way again, a vehicle barrier bears a Forest Enterprise notice declaring that walkers are welcome here!

Turn left along the road for 150 yards, then turn right and follow a path, bending to the right at first and maintaining height. The view beyond the radio mast is of the Cranborne Chase and Shaftesbury uplands. With tumuli on the right, angle down to the left in the direction of Winterborne Houghton. The grass gives way to a track which passes through a gate and then descends steeply. Turn left on to a tarmac track up to, and through, Higher Houghton Farm – at the last dwelling you may be greeted by peacocks. Go through a gate and walk up the long, green valley of Heath Bottom. Enter woods by a gate and start to climb… and climb. Go through a gate and up steeply into a field. Here go up and slightly right, aiming for a water trough near which is a gate on to a road. Turn left to return to **Bulbarrow Hill** and the car park.

POINTS OF INTEREST:

Milton Abbey – As early as the 10th century there was an abbey here, though the present building is mainly from the 14th and 15th centuries. The nave was never completed, perhaps because of the Dissolution, after which Henry VIII disposed of the estate to Sir John Tregonwell, an ancestor of the founder of Bournemouth. Joseph Damer bought the property in 1752 and built his mansion in 1771, incorporating the old Abbot's Hall with its fine interior timber roof. The house is now a public school. Limited viewing is permitted at Easter and in the summer holidays. The Abbey is open daily.

Bulbarrow Hill – At 902 feet (275m), the hill is second in eminence in the county only to Pilsdon Pen. From it the view extends westward over the Vale of Blackmore as far as the Quantocks and the Mendips in Somerset.

REFRESHMENTS:
The Hambros Arms, Milton Abbas.
Tea Clipper, Milton Abbas (light lunches and cream teas).

Walk 93 WINTERBORNES AND COMBS DITCH 8¹/₂m (13¹/₂km)

Maps: OS Sheets Landranger 194 and 195; Pathfinder 1319 and 1300.

Moderate going through fields, woods and villages.

Start: At 863976, by Winterborne Kingston church.

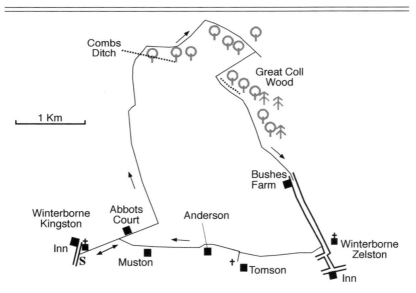

Leave the village along East Street at the back of the church and by the farm buildings, take the blue-waymarked bridleway parallel to the Abbot's Court drive. Continue through flat fields to a steel gate and bend left with the track 150 yards beyond it. About ¹/₂ mile further on, go through a 'garden gate' on to a covered path. Pass a stile on the left and eventually emerge at a large field: keep left, then bend right at the top of it. Turn left at a small gate, go past a collapsed barn and, after joining a grassy track, reach the top of the ridge by a reservoir. Cross the line of **Combs Ditch** – seen more impressively later on – and go half-right. Pass a large track on the right, but do not turn right until you are level with a gate. The path joins a larger track and bends left by some enormous beech trees. It then continues to a junction: turn right along the back of some woods. Walk for over ¹/₂ mile and, shortly after a depression with a private turning, look for a bridleway to the right – not shown on the Landranger map. The way leads to a large field: keep left and go up to a gate in the corner. Here is Combs Ditch again – on both sides.

Turn left and walk along the far side of a wood with the clearly visible Ditch running parallel, but inside. At a gate, enter Great Coll Wood, but continue in the same direction through the great variety of broad-leaved trees with conifers in the background and, in their season, acres of bluebells. At the end of the wood, carry on across a field – Charborough Tower is ahead – and go through two gates. Go past Bushes Farm and down a road to lovely **Winterborne Zelston**. Just before the church, turn right (for the inn, go over the bridge and soon turn left up to the main road – a total of $^1/_4$ mile. Return to this point). Go along a short lane and then follow a path on the left side of the fields. Do a left and a right through a farmyard and then go straight along a farm road to reach a T-junction. Turn left to visit **Winterborne Tomson**, just 200 yards away. Return to a stile by the junction. Go over and cross a field, aiming just to the left of the largest tree on the far side. Keep to the left of the next two fields, passing the back of **(Winterborne) Anderson**. Turn left where a track crosses and turn right after a further 150 yards into an area of farm buildings. Turn right again through the yard, then go left to reach a gate and stile at the end of the concrete. Follow the path beyond to the right through fields and over stiles to reach **Winterborne Muston** Manor. Turn right along the driveway, right again at the farm and immediately left over a stile. Keep to the left side of the next field to reach the road back to Winterborne Kingston.

POINTS OF INTEREST:
Combs Ditch – Like the more famous Bokerley Dyke (*see* Note to Walk 96), this is a defensive bank and ditch. It was long thought to date from Romano-British times, but excavations in 1965 suggested an earlier (Iron Age) construction.
The Winterborne villages – **Zelston** is named after Henry de Seles, a 14th-century lord of the manor. **Tomson** has a 12th-century church with a single nave and chancel and a Georgian oak interior. Its manor dates from the early 17th century. The Winterborne prefix is usually omitted from **Anderson** nowadays. The Manor was built in 1622 for John Tregonwell III of Milton Abbas. **Muston** Manor is a large, early 18th-century house.

REFRESHMENTS:
The Botany Bay Inne, Winterborne Zelston.
The Greyhound Inn, Winterborne Kingston.

Walk 94   TURNWORTH AND IBBERTON $8^1/_2$m ($13^1/_2$km)

Maps: OS Sheets Landranger 14, Pathfinder 1280 and 1281.
A marvellous downland walk near Blandford Forum.
Start: At 811094, the car park/picnic area on Okeford Hill.

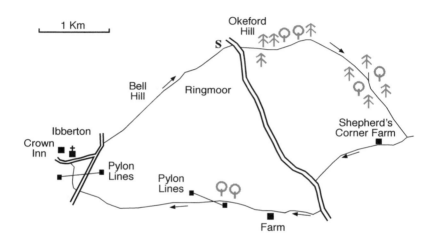

The starting car park is at the top of Okeford Hill, on the road from Okeford Fitzpaine to Turnworth and on to Winterbourne Whitechurch.

From the start on **Okeford Hill** take the bridleway across the road, heading eastwards. Go into woodland and ignore all side turnings to arrive at a trig. point close to where the track forks. Bear right to swing around the trig. point. Follow the track across open land, heading towards more woodland. Ignore a crossing track to enter the woods. Where a track joins from the left, turn right. Now ignore side turnings, passing an old hut to the left. Continue along the track, bearing right to go through a gate, then following a hedge, to the left. Go through another gate and continue to reach a lane. Turn right along the lane to reach Shepherd's Corner Farm.

Take the track ahead, going between the farm buildings and climbing gently to reach a track junction. Go straight ahead, descending to reach a road. To the right,

178

along the road is **Turnworth**. However, our route goes left, following the road for 500 yards to reach a farm access lane on the right. Take this, following it to the farm and taking a waymarked track westward. Soon the track peters out: continue ahead, keeping to the right of two clumps of woodland and going under the pylon lines to cross several fields. Across these a gate is reached, beyond which the bridleway becomes more obvious, crossing the downland in a fine position with open views on all sides. Follow the track to a road on Ibberton Hill.

There is now a choice. The shorter way is to go right along the road, but this misses a detour to the refreshment stop at Ibberton. So cross the road and continue along a path that bears half-right across a field, then follows the left edge of another to reach a gate on to a road. Cross and follow the path opposite to reach **Ibberton Church** and the Crown Inn. After your visit to these fine sites, return to the road and turn left along it, going steeply up to reach a road junction. Turn left for 200 yards, then go right, off the road, along a ridge track on top of Bell Hill. Follow this past **Ringmoor**, to the right, and the picnic area, to the left, to rejoin the start.

POINTS OF INTEREST:

Okeford Hill – Okeford is an old beacon hill, a beacon having been lit here to announce the sighting of the Spanish Armada (in 1588) and on the 400th anniversary of the sighting in 1988.

Turnworth – The church here was rebuilt in 1869 by G R Crickmay, though the architect's assistant, one Thomas Hardy, is rather better known. Hardy designed the capitals and corbels.

Ibberton Church – The Church of St Eustace is one of only three in England dedicated to the Roman general Eustachius.

Ringmoor – The National Trust owns this site of a Celtic/Romano – British settlement. The views from the track past the site are breathtaking.

REFRESHMENTS:
The Crown Inn, Ibberton.

Walk 95   **ASHMORE WOOD**   9m (14^1/$_2$km)

Maps: OS Sheets Landranger 184 and 195; Pathfinder 1281.

A magnificent walk in Cranborne Chase.

Start: At 913178, the duck pond in Ashmore.

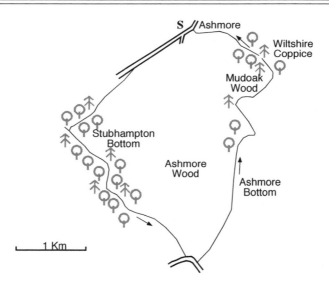

From the duck pond go westward along the village street, passing the war memorial and church, and heading towards Fontmell Magna. The road descends towards a 'single track' sign. Just before this go left, through a gate, and bear right across a field to reach a gate at the left end of some conifers. Go through and soon turn left over a stile. Turn right, following the hedge to reach a stile in it. Go over this and turn left along the hedge to reach a gate. Go through and walk forward to reach a crossing track. Turn left, following the track through the wood. At a clearing, when a track joins from the left, turn right on a path that descends to reach a crossing track in **Stubhampton Bottom**.

Turn left along the Bottom, ignoring all side turnings for 2 miles to reach a blue waymarker pointing left into a field. Go not follow this: instead, walk forward to reach a lane. Follow this to reach a signed bridleway on the left. This bridleway goes through Ashmore Bottom, passing through several gates to reach a gate into woodland (another section of Ashmore Wood). Go through and turn right, as waymarked, going uphill to reach a crossing track. Turn left along this track to reach a yellow waymarker pointing rightwards along a track that runs between a hedge and a fence. Take this, bearing right to follow the southern edge of Mudoak Wood to a gate. Go through and turn left along a track that goes downhill to reach a stile. Go over and follow the right edge of the field beyond to reach a stile on the right. Go over and turn left along a path. Where this forks take the right branch, going through Wiltshire Copse. The path itself is the border between Dorset and Wiltshire.

Go over a stile and walk forward to reach another. Go over and follow a path to reach another stile on the left. Go over this and follow a path to reach a gate near a house. Go through and follow the track beyond to a lane. Turn right into **Ashmore**, taking a last few steps to return to the duck pond.

POINTS OF INTEREST:
Stubhampton Bottom – This superb, steep-sided, wooded valley offers one of the best walks in Dorset, with flowers and butterflies galore in spring and summer, and deer for the very lucky visitor.
Ashmore – This beautiful village, with thatched cottages grouped around a large duck pond, is the highest in Dorset, over 700 feet above sea level.

REFRESHMENTS:
None on the route, but available at Tollard Royal, to the east of Ashmore, and Tarrant Gunville, to the south.

Walk 96   BOKERLEY DYKE AND CRANBORNE   10m (16km)

Maps: OS Sheets Landranger 184 and 195; Pathfinder 1282.
Ancient earthworks and fine open country.
Start: At 034178, Pentridge Church.

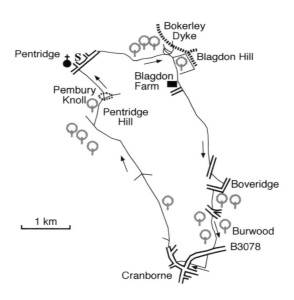

From the church, return to the road, turn left and walk to the top of the hamlet. At a farm, turn right up a stony lane which, after the first of two steel gates, becomes grassy. Follow the lane around the shoulder of a hill, then bend left through another gate. Pass a wood on the left and start a gradual descent, with an excellent view on the left across to the Ox Drove ridge. Pass through a small beech wood and turn right after going through a small gate. Now continue for 80 yards to join a stony farm track. Here you can make a short, but worthwhile, diversion. On the left, just inside the edge of a wood, a thin path winds gently uphill for 400 yards to reach Blagdon Hill. On emerging from the wood, the walker is startled by a spectacular view of **Bokerley Dyke** down to the left. After due admiration of the antiquities and the hilltop views, retrace your steps to the main route.

Turn left down the farm track to Blagdon Farm, continuing on the surfaced lane for about a mile to reach a minor road. Turn right along the road and, after 200 yards, go left on to a track. Next, turn right up a slope into the hamlet of Boveridge. Turn right along a road for 150 yards, then go left up the edge of a wood. Go through a gate and cross a field to reach a stile in the right-hand corner. The old church here is now a private residence. Follow the road to Damerham for 100 yards, then turn right over a stile into Burwood. Bear left at a large clearing and head southward through old and new woodland to reach a road (the B3078). Turn right, then immediately left into a field. At the bottom of the field turn right, then go second left into Penny's Mead, opposite the sports field. Turn right along the near side of the stream into **Cranborne**, a suitable place for refreshments.

Leave Cranborne by the far end of The Square, turning right. Fork left after 350 yards, following a rising metalled road which soon becomes a track. The track bends and undulates lightly for about 2 miles to reach a col at the side of Pentridge Hill. Fork right after a gate, heading towards the hill itself. Along the terrace walk the views extend west to the wooded Cranborne Chase and south-west to the eminence of Bulbarrow, while in the summit wood on **Pembury Knoll**, the walker can enjoy the purple foxgloves or shelter from the freezing wind, each at its time of year. From the top, go left from your approach line, heading down the north-west ridge towards Pentridge church in the trees below. There is no clear path at first, but further down aim for the left end of a row of sycamores to reach a narrow waymarked path that leads down to a road. Now walk a few yards right and then turn left for the church and start point.

POINTS OF INTEREST:
Bokerley Dyke – This three-mile bank and ditch was built by the Romano-British early in the 4th century. It was extended and strengthened later that century as a defence against warring tribes.
Cranborne – This was once the administrative centre of Cranborne Chase. In Thomas Hardy's *Tess of the d'Urbervilles*, Cranborne is portrayed as Chaseborough.
Pembury Knoll – The knoll is topped by an Iron Age hill fort.

REFRESHMENTS:
The Fleur de Lys, Cranborne. This inn was Hardy's 'Flower de Luce'.
The Sheaf of Arrows, Cranborne.

Walk 97 BADBURY RINGS AND TARRANT CRAWFORD   10m (16km)
Maps: OS Sheets Landranger 195; Pathfinder 1300.
Spacious landscape, a gem of a church and the mighty Rings.
Start: At 962032, the National Trust car park, Badbury Rings.

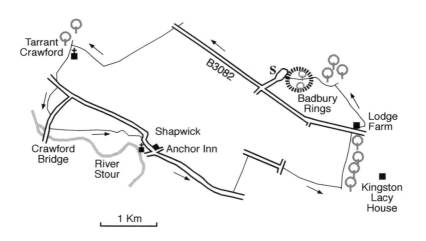

N.B. Dogs are not permitted within Badbury Rings itself at any time. An alternative final section of this walk is provided for those walking with dogs.

Return to the road and turn right along the wide green strip through the Avenue of Beeches. At its end, cross the road carefully and follow the verge for about 400 yards, then turn left for Tarrant Crawford. After a mile, turn right on a stony track which rises, then descends. Turn left alongside a stream, soon reaching **Tarrant Crawford Church**. Beyond the church, and level with the first farm buildings, climb a stile on the left and cross a field to reach another stile beside a gate. The track beyond angles upwards behind Tarrant Abbey House, then crosses a field. Go over a road and keep right in the next field. Cross a tarmac track and pass beneath power lines to reach the last of the stiles in this section of the walk. Cross the field aiming just to the right of the next pylon to reach a gate on to the road. Turn right and walk to the medieval Crawford Bridge, here spanning two streams of the River Stour. The village over the bridge is Spetisbury.

Retrace a hundred or so steps and turn right over a stile into the river meadows (which can be very wet in winter). Head east across a field, aiming just left of a distant cluster of trees to reach a stile. Go over to reach the riverside. As the river bends right, leave it and cross a field to a stile in the middle of the fence. Do the same in the next field, then keep left of a solitary oak to reach a gate in the corner of the field. Follow the track beyond into Shapwick (pronounced Shappick). The Anchor Inn is at the cross-roads. Now walk along Stewards Lane for a mile, then turn left along a metalled track. Pass between farm buildings and turn right at a road. At a T-junction, go across on to a bridleway. After $3/4$ mile, turn left at a T-junction. Through the woods on the right is **Kingston Lacy**: continue to the B3082 and cross with care.

At this point, those with dogs should turn left and walk for about a mile beside the beeches, then turn right to return to the car park.

Go past **Lodge Farm**, through a gate and follow a path which bends left, gaining height through two fields to reach a wood at the top. Turn left and skirt the wood. Now go to the right of a facing gate and over the stile into Badbury Rings. The starting car park is on the far, west, side of the site.

POINTS OF INTEREST:

St Mary's Church, Tarrant Crawford – A mostly 12th-century building with a tiled gable topping the tower. Inside there are 13th-century wall paintings and two coffin lids of the same period - of Queen Joan of Scotland, daughter of King John, and of Richard Poore, Bishop of Salisbury (1217-28). The church is now redundant, but remains consecrated.

Kingston Lacy – The house, designed by Sir Roger Platt, was built for Sir Ralph Bankes in 1663-65. Among the treasures within are paintings by Rubens, Van Dyck, Breughel, Lely and Romney. The house has been administered by the National Trust since 1981.

Lodge Farm – A 14th-century hunting lodge probably built for John of Gaunt, father of Henry IV.

REFRESHMENTS:
The Anchor Inn, Shapwick.

Walk 98 DANCING LEDGE AND WORTH MATRAVERS 10m (16km)
Maps: OS Sheets Landranger 195; Outdoor Leisure 15.
A very undulating coastal walk with fine views.
Start: At 033773, Durlston Country Park car park.

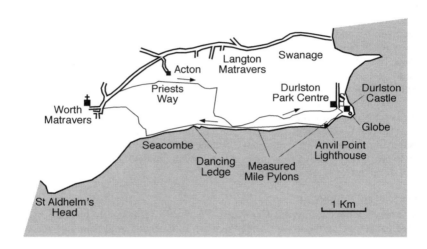

Leaving the car park, take the road down to Durlston Castle, pass it on the left and continue downwards to the viewing position. Here one can safely watch the sea birds on the cliff side (about 50 yards to the left is the Great Globe). From the viewing position, follow the path westwards along the cliff to Tilly Whim Caves (closed). Note the two **measured nautical mile pylons** immediately above the caves. The path now descends, then rises steeply and passes on the seaward side of Anvil Point Lighthouse (closed). The path continues westward: follow the sign for the Coast Path over a stile into the National Trust Belle Vue Estate and over another stile at the end of the Estate near the other measured nautical mile pylons. Keep following the boundary fence along the cliff, passing over several more stiles to reach Dancing Ledge, a former quarry. Continue westwards, over a stile, following the stone waymark Coastal Path and Seacombe. On descending into the Seacombe inlet, turn immediately inland and

186

proceed up the valley bottom. A stone waymark for Worth is passed. Later, a post points half-left to Worth. Walk up a long field to a stile, go over and climb up the next steep field to a signpost that can be seen at the top. Take the path straight ahead, stone waymarked 'Worth $^1/_2$', over the crown of the hill. Go over a stile and across the final field and passage-way into **Worth Matravers**.

Keeping to the right, leave the centre of the village and, after 100 yards, at the junction beneath the Square and Compass Inn, take the right fork. Continue on the road, and after passing the last houses on the right, go over the stile signposted 'Swanage 4'. Cross two fields signposted Eastington and Priest's Way and go over a stone stile signposted 'Priest's Way and Swanage $3^1/_2$'. In about $^1/_2$ mile, the hamlet of Acton is reached on the left. Continue along Priest's Way. Langton Matravers is on the left. Pass the stone waymark to Dancing Ledge and Spyway, then go through a gate and turn right at the second stone waymark for Dancing Ledge and Coast. Proceed along the left-hand side of a field and the right-hand side of subsequent fields. The path descends steeply and there are seaward views. At the bottom field, the path goes right, then through a hedge, to join another. Turn left to pick up the eastbound coastal path again. After crossing two springs, the path divides (no signpost). Take the track which gradually rises up the Downs and go over a stile with a red and white marker post. The path now contours the Down, passing above the measured nautical mile pylons. Climb gradually up two fields to a stile on to Round Down and walk to a gate into Durlston Country Park (*see* Note to Walk 20). Here, turn half-left into an area of pasture and gorse bushes. Maintain direction and go through the first gate on the right. Pass through a small, then later a large, gate. Anvil Point Lighthouse now comes into view. The path joins the road from the lighthouse and leads back to the car park.

POINTS OF INTEREST:
Measured Nautical Mile Pylons – These are used by the Admiralty for speed trials.
Worth Matravers – An attractive stone village with pond and village green. The clergy of St Nicholas' church here originally walked to Swanage along the Priest's Way, to officiate.

REFRESHMENTS:
The Square and Compass Inn, Worth Matravers.
There are also tea-rooms in Worth Matravers.

Walk 99   CORFE CASTLE AND KIMMERIDGE   10m (16km)

Maps: OS Sheets Landranger 195; Outdoor Leisure 15.

A strenuous walk with splendid views.

Start: At 959825, the National Trust car park, Corfe Castle.

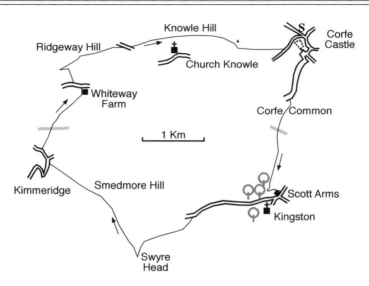

Leave the car park by following the main road around the base of the castle. On entering **Corfe Castle** square, follow the pavement around past the National Trust shop and exit on the far side. In $^1/_2$ mile, at the end of the village, go over the cattle grid and follow the roadway, disregarding the signpost to Kingston, for a further 100 yards into a dip. Almost immediately turn half-left and pick up a grassy track over the Common which leads to the crest of the hill. Continue in the same direction and descend to a footbridge and stile. This is hidden among the bushes and can best be located by noting, from the hilltop, where the path across the next two fields exits from the bridge. Having crossed the two fields go over a stile into a fairly overgrown and often muddy defile with a stream alongside. This opens up into a footpath that climbs steeply up three fields almost to Kingston. At the top, turn right up a wooded lane and, almost immediately, left in front of some cottages. Continue and turn right at the end. The walker is now by the car park and garden of the Scott Arms Hotel. Almost immediately, turn right up the main street of Kingston, passing the church on the left. Continue along the road for $3/4$ mile to a small car park and private road on the left. Here take the path which goes up the field, with a wood on your right-hand side. Later, there is a delightful view of Endcombe House and the Golden Bowl below. At the summit, **Swyre Head**, go over a stile and stand near the tumuli to admire the view.

Return over the stile and walk westwards, waymarked Kimmeridge, by the stone wall of the escarpment for $1^{1}/_{2}$ miles. Where the path meets a road, turn left and at the junction almost immediately ahead turn right. (On the opposite side of the road is a stile and signpost 'Kimmeridge $1/_{4}$'. To visit **Kimmeridge**, go down the steep field and take the path by the side of the churchyard. Return by this route to rejoin the walk.) The road runs a short distance along a ridge: look out for a waymarked path on the right which starts on the crest about 50 yards from the junction. Go down the steep field, over a bridge and stile, and follow a path diagonally across the next three large fields to reach a gate in the top right-hand corner by Whiteway Farm. Here, turn left along a track to a road. Turn left up the road for 100 yards, then go up the lane on the right. In about a further 100 yards, take the waymarked route to the left, going through a field and leaving a sheet metal barn on the right. At the top of the field, which is at the base of Ridgeway Hill, turn left up a well-defined track to reach a gate after 150 yards. Turn sharp right and follow the track up a steep hill. At the top, turn right and follow the path which crosses a minor road above the hamlet of Cocknowle and then climbs over Knowle Hill, from which there are extensive views inland. The path shortly starts to descend the south side of the hill and, after $3/4$ mile, reaches a road. Turn left and follow the road by the base of the castle back to the car park.

POINTS OF INTEREST:
Corfe Castle – An attractive stone village dominated by the ruins of the Castle. It was given to the National Trust as part of the Bankes Bequest.
Swyre Head – At 666 feet, the highest point in Purbeck.
Kimmeridge – This attractive village of stone and thatch is part of the Smedmore Estate.

REFRESHMENTS:
The Scott Arms, Kingston.
Post Office, Kimmeridge.
There are various inns and cafés in Corfe Castle.

Walk 100 CRANBORNE AND GUSSAGE ALL SAINTS 13m (21km)
Maps: OS Sheets Landranger 184 and 195; Pathfinder 1281 and 1282.

Rolling chalk uplands and a Roman road.

Start: At 057134, the car park at Water Street, Cranborne.

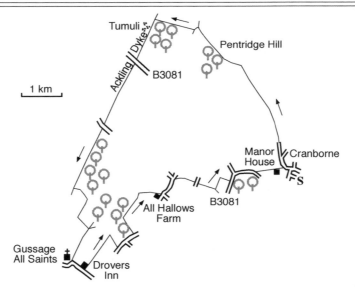

Cross the main road into The Square and turn right at its far end. Walk up the road for 350 yards, then fork left up a rising lane. This soon becomes a grassy track winding gently up and down through farmland for about 2 miles. At a col beside Pentridge Hill, go through a gate and bear left and down. The view ahead is of wooded Cranborne Chase with Bulbarrow away to the south-west. Keep left, go through a gate and down a rough track. At the bottom, turn left - it can be very wet here - and after 100 yards turn right into a field. In the next field (which can be skirted if it is under plough or crop), the path goes half-left over the brow of a hill to reach the far corner of woods: go down to some elderly waymarked gates and turn left.

You are now walking along a Roman road, **Ackling Dyke**, which passes tumuli on the right and a wood on the left. Go over a road (the B3081), just beyond which is

190

a Roman milestone. The raised path now continues arrow-straight until it is blocked by trees. Drop down and follow the same line, going to the left of the trees. The path crosses a minor road and then rises gradually through woodland, passing a commemorative stone to John Ironmonger, agent to the Earl of Shaftesbury. Beyond the wood, the path continues to rise: about 200 yards past the highest point, go left, as waymarked, along the line of a hedge. The route now leaves Ackling Dyke, which heads for Badbury Rings on the horizon. Further to the left is Horton Tower. The new path bends right, then right again and becomes broader. Turn left at the bottom of a slope and go right at a junction of farm tracks to reach the church in Gussage. Turn left through the village to reach the Drovers Inn.

Turn left and up by the inn, following the path as it widens and reaches a vehicle barrier and T-junction. Turn right, then left at the road. Follow the road for about 500 yards and then turn left on a wide stony lane in a wooded belt. Next, follow a waymarker into a field on the right. Keep to the left side of the first field and the right side of the second and at a major stony track, turn right to All Hallows Farm. Turn left on to the road, go over a stream and, at a left-hand bend in the road, turn off right. Instantly right again on to a track, tunnel-like at first, which rises slightly as it heads east. Cross a narrow metalled lane and continue on the grassy track until there is a left turn, then a right turn. Follow this to reach a barn beside the B3081.

Turn left along the road, then go right towards Cranborne. After 500 yards, at a small stony lay-by, cross a stile and go diagonally across a field. Three stiles and a footbridge later, turn right to see the fine building of **Cranborne Manor**. Either of the gates at the end of the meadow leads back into Cranborne.

POINTS OF INTEREST:

Ackling Dyke – This Roman road ran between Sorviodunum (Salisbury) and Durnovaria (Dorchester). The section followed by the walk is one of the best preserved, with the central causeway and side ditches clearly visible.

Cranborne Manor – The manor was originally built in the 13th century as a hunting lodge, but was extended and improved early in the 17th century by Robert Cecil, 1st Earl of Salisbury. It is not open to the public. The gardens, laid out by John Tradescant, are open occasionally. The village church dates from the 13th century and contains some famous medieval wall paintings.

REFRESHMENTS:
Fleur de Lys, Cranborne.
The Sheaf of Arrows, Cranborne.
The Drovers Inn, Gussage All Saints.

Titles in the Series

Buckinghamshire and Hertfordshire

Cambridgeshire and Bedfordshire

County Durham

Devon and Cornwall

Dorset

Greater London

Northumberland

Somerset and Avon

Staffordshire

Surrey

Warwickshire and the West Midlands

West Sussex